# D. U. K. W.s TO WATER

*by*

**PETER R. DYER**

To Ian,
very best wishes on your 80th Birthday

Hoping you enjoy my book

Regards. [signature] 18/05/2020
(author)

TotalRecall Publications, Inc..
1103 Middlecreek
Friendswood,  Texas  77546
281-992-3131 TL
www.totalrecallpress.com





Printed in the United States of America with simultaneously
printings in Australia, Canada, and United Kingdom.
FIRST EDITION
1   2   3   4   5   6   7   8   9   10

### To Mum, Dad my family and Smartie my old, white cat!

This story is dedicated to all those individuals who have served on the wind-blown beaches of the North-West of England aboard the WW II veteran amphibious rescue vehicles known as the duck (D.U.K.W.).It is dedicated on behalf of the over 600 individuals, not to mention animals, who owe their lives to the presence of the lifeguard crews in their yellow and red painted rescue craft. It was for a period of not quite five decades, from 1951 to 1998, this unique partnership of man and machine struggled to make the coastline of Britain, between Preston and Liverpool, a safer environment to either carry out coastal commercial activities, or to just enjoy as a citizen or visitor.

Amongst the many interesting and helpful people whom it has been an honour to encounter during my research into this untold story, I must mention in particular the name of the late Bill Doherty who died in 1998. Bill was the last of the great lifeguards and guardians of our shoreline. His personal notes and records are the glue which holds this account together. I must also thank his widow Pat and the Doherty family for allowing me access to those documents. It is my great personal regret that Bill did not live to see the conclusion of this moderate endeavour.

I must also mention in particular my good friend Laurie Hardman. His literary skills fashioned a rough plank of a manuscript into a polished publication I hope worthy of the heroes who live within its pages.

My thanks also to my good friend Charles O'Hara for getting me over all the technical difficulties of delivering this work to the publisher specifications.

During my research, I spoke to many individuals whose stories have been the inspiration for this publication. There are many more, however, whom I did not have the pleasure of encountering. Amongst those individuals, I am sure, there are many whose experiences were just as interesting and worthy.

Finally my thanks to my publisher Bruce Moran.

**Peter Dyer (2019)**

# Acknowledgements

**This book would not have been possible without the
invaluable contribution of the following individuals and organisations.**

- The late Bill Doherty (deputy Chief Lifeguard Southport/ Sefton MBC 1966 to 1991/ Chief Lifeguard 1991 to 1997)
- Keith Hick (For his invaluable and skilled advice)
- The Late Verdi Godwin (Chief Lifeguard Southport/ Sefton MBC 1958 to 1991)
- Pat Doherty (widow of Bill Doherty)
- The late Joseph Rankin RNR (shrimper, D.U.K.W. entrepreneur)
- Rob Routledge (grandson of John Routledge.)
- Chris Trees (master mechanic, Thompson and Doxey
- Export and Sefton MBC)
- Roger Cocker (Lifeguard Sefton MBC)
- Tony Venturini (D.U.K.W. driver Southport/ Sefton MBC)
- Darren Twist (Lifeguard Sefton MBC)
- The late Phil King (Head of Leisure Services Southport/ Sefton)
- David McAleavy (director Coast and Countryside Service, Sefton MBC)
- Chris Jones (Ex-beach superintendent Southport/ Sefton MBC)
- Rod Taylor (apprentice Mechanical Engineer Thompson/Doxey
- The staff of the Southport Atkinson Library Margaret Biddolph
- The staff of the New Brighton Library
- Paul Shunke (D.U.K.W. driver and Lifeguard Sefton MBC)
- The staff of St. Ann's Reference library
- Peter Jelley (research material)
- Christine and Paul McGannon (relatives of the late Arthur McGannon)
- Jim Taylor Beach Superintendent and Ranger)
- Kelley Thompson (London D.U.K.W. Tours)
- Matt Watts London Duck Tours
- James Butcher Rexfeatures
- James Biddolph family
- Trinity/Mirror Publishing LTD Reflections Photo Archive

The author has tried his best to credit the images contained in this publication to their correct owners. His extreme apology to any image he has incorrectly credited.

The author has done his best to obtain the necessary copyrights of all images of which he was aware of, held under copyrights, at the time of publication.

# Table of Contents

Southport's First (unofficial) Coat of Arms.
Note: Lifeboat image later removed.

# THIS BOOK
### Recognition of contributors.
### Interviews/images.

**JP Author's 1942 Ford/Willys' Jeep and D. U. K. W.**

'Greater Love has no man than this, that he lays down his life for a friend....'
**--John 15**

**Before the D.U.K.W. there was the lifeboat"**
**The Southport self-righting lifeboat Mary Anna 1888"**

'The D.U.K.W. was a metal Sheepdog.' Chief Lifeguard Bill Doherty 1995.

**--Sefton M.B.C.**

"Rescue DUKW no 20 has arrived to save another life."

# Introduction

**D**uring the bleak Post war year of 1949, the Curator of a small and rather unknown local museum, in a typically sleepy English seaside town, began to write down his memories. These were recollections of the men and the Lifeboats he had witnessed from his youth, that once had graced that part of England's dune lined coastline. Under oil lamp and in the daylight hours, he drew on every letter, report and record on the dusty shelves of his beloved Botanic Gardens Museum in the small Lancashire seaside town of Southport. Finally, before he died, J H Lawson Booth managed to complete his second book, *A History of The Southport Lifeboats*. It was the last dedicated act that his failing health allowed. The devoted Curator was able to bequest his book both to the Museum and consequently, to the town he loved.

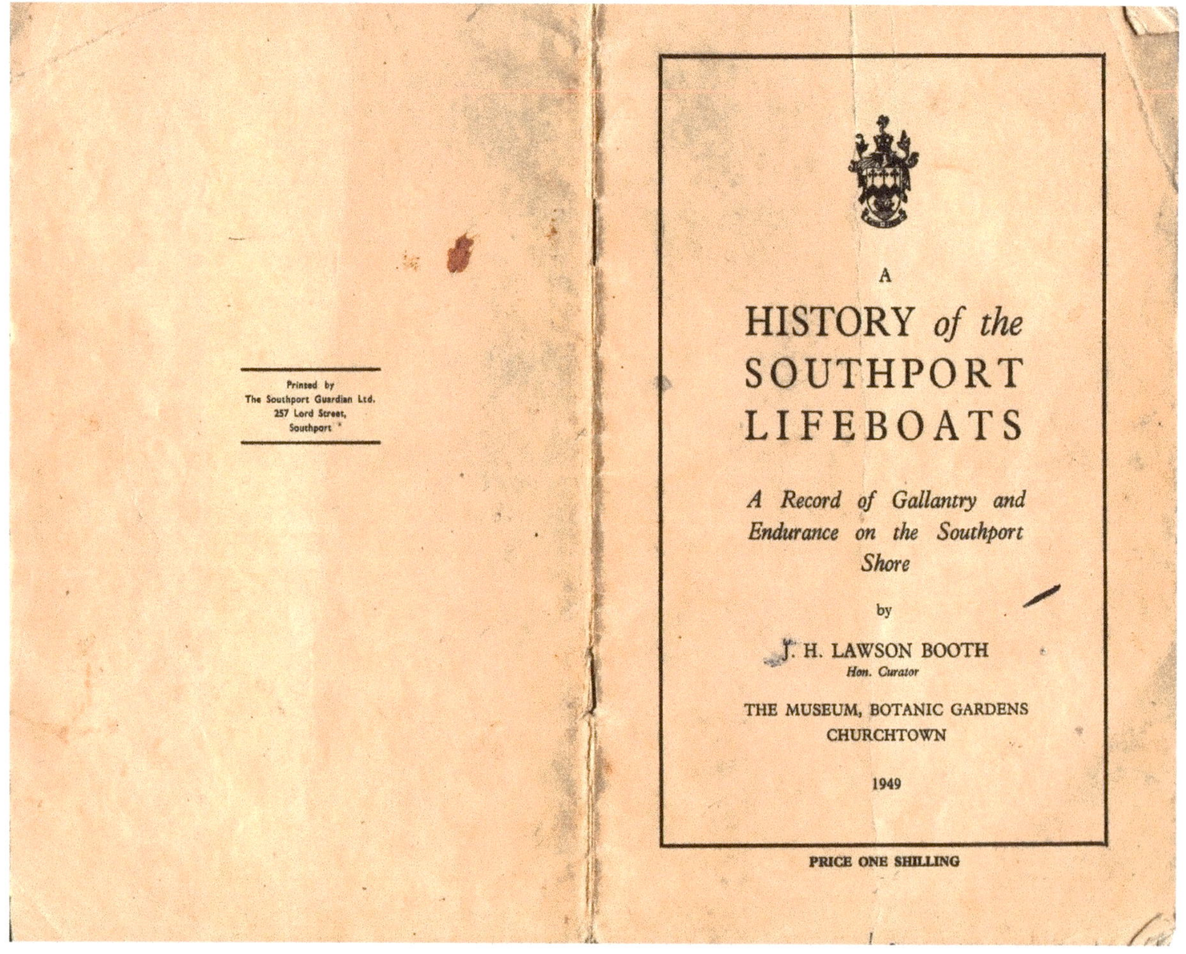


Lawson booth

Lawson Booth's final great endeavour complemented his earlier work, *Sea Casualties of The Southport Coast* which he finished only a year or so prior to the ending of the local Lifeboat service. Together they formed a valuable focus on a moment in our maritime history, but more important the recognition of the courage and sacrifice of those who face the wrath of the sea to rescue others in danger.

Lawson Booth had been driven by one great desire. Not to let the heroic endeavours of the Lifeboat service go unrecorded and thus become forgotten with the passing of time. This desire became even more sharpened as Southport's Lifeboat station was finally closed in 1925 and with it much of the physical evidence of those heroic times. Booth was only too aware that all the remaining evidence and records of those countless acts of selfless bravery could, at any time in the future, could be lost forever. He seems to have been a man who could foresee the fragile nature of the survival of our authority run local museums and libraries! Booth, however, acted just in time. His publication recorded for posterity details of the ships, the crews, the cargoes, the rescues and the individuals who battled against the might of the sea along our coast from 1786 to 1925. Ironically, the aging curator would not have been aware that within two years of his *History of The Southport Lifeboats* rolling off the press, a new coastal rescue service was to emerge to guard that very same shoreline. By 1949, however, the open lifeboat, with its stout oars, pulled by oilskin clad crews, drawn from the ranks of local fishermen and volunteers, had long disappeared into the mists of memory. Equally, the coloured rockets that lit the black night sky, bringing hope to the crews of countless beleaguered vessels in mortal peril. Gone also the huge horses panting clouds of vapour as they dragged those creaking lifeboats to the launching position in thundering waves.

In 1949 came a vehicle not originally designed for the saving of lives! The United States WW II Amphibious D.U.K.W. was a machine born of and built for war. It was specifically designed to supply and transport military materials and personnel engaged in that bloodiest of all wars, the Second World War. The military specifications for this Ex US army two and a half-ton swimming truck, therefore, may have seemed to make this revolutionary vehicle a very unlikely candidate to fill the role as a life saving craft. But as we shall see, that is exactly how the hand of fate was to play in this Maritime tale. .The story of the amphibious D.U.K.W. in its post WW II service, is a true " Swords to Ploughshares" tale. It is one that I hope you will find as fascinating to read as it has been for me to explore and so pass on to you.

Artwork: Author

# CHAPTER ONE

# THE TIME, THE PLACE

For the location of the following events we must travel to the North West coast of England, approximately 15 miles north of the historic and commercially busy city of Liverpool. This stretch of Britain's coastline has been famous from the great days of commercial sailing, to fishing and shrimping. In the 1700s the local invention of the bathing machine heralded a new, and economically much loved individual, the leisure seeker! The fortunes of many of Britains' small seaside towns was transformed by the holiday maker who still contributes much to local economies right up to this present day.

For as long as the Irish sea has lapped the once sandy beaches of our destination, the seemingly idyllic coastline had a darker reputation. Its placid waters can quickly be transformed by powerful South Westerly, storm shrouded winds. Beneath apparently friendly, flat, sandy beaches lie ship- wrecking sandbanks and the dangerous attention of hidden quick-sands! Countless are the lives which this combination of nature's minefields has snatched, especially from the ranks of distressed vessels of all shapes and sizes together with individuals who were both local and strangers to this stretch of the South Lancashire coastline.

Enter then a lumbering six wheeled vehicle, fresh from far away encounters which tested to the limit the concept of a machine that could crawl out of the sea and then work equally well on land.

This is a saga of the sea never before related except from the very lips of those who were the leading actors in this drama. As if to mirror the very fears of Lawson Booth, no other record survives dedicated to those who, aboard their steel hulled D.U.K.W.s, served this community. They, however, truly followed in the wake of Lawson Booth's Warriors of the Sea, and truly shared in the fortunes of that same, dangerous dedication.

It is now some two or more decades since the last red and yellow painted D.U.W.K.s patrolled the beaches of Southport, Ainsdale and Birkdale. For those people who witnessed the deep rumbling engine, the whine of the tyres on sand, the rattling of the gearbox, those days are also in the past but unlike its predecessor the self-righting lifeboat, their legacy is still a very recent event. There are many for whom their first meeting with the six wheeled amphibian is more than a simple memory. There are over 600 holiday makers, fishermen, yacht crews, wind-surfers, would-be suicides and (yes animals), who have a much clearer memory of those servants of the sea. They are the ones who owe their lives to the rescue DUWKs and their vigilant crews. Their story it is my honour and privilege to tell to you. Let us then 'Switch on the engine!' engage the propeller! We enter the ocean of time, where this saga of the sea begins.

**THE D.U.K.W. HAS TAKEN TO WATER!**

# CHAPTER TWO

# THE UGLY DUCKLING GOES TO WAR

On the northern point of the Horn of Massachusetts, upon the Eastern seaboard of the United States, lies a small, though busy coastal town named Provincetown. Far away across the fierce Atlantic Ocean, many miles from the coast of Northern Britain, there was born a vehicle that would transcend international boundaries when it came to the business of rescuing human beings from the grip of dangerous seas.

1942: On the sandy, sloping beach of that small East coast American town-ship, lay a revolutionary machine the invention of which is the starting point of this story. The United States had just had a major wake-up call when its whole Pacific fleet was almost destroyed during a surprise attack by the carrier born aircraft of the Japanese Imperial Navy. For the first time in its short history, America's coastline was under serious threat from a well-armed and fanatical enemy. The American Government, led by Democratic President Franklin D. Roosevelt, soon became aware that many military problems had to be surmounted before the US armed forces could turn the tide against those of the Japanese Imperial Empire.

This strange grey, half truck, half boat that stood in a yard just off the Provincetown beach was the proposed solution to some of those very pressing problems confronting the United States armed forces. The revolutionary amphibious vehicle's operational future, however, was far from certain, and on that day in 1942 all indications were that the duck vehicle was heading for the scrap heap of history.

All had seemed to be going positively in the vehicle's initial development. The military problem she was invented to solve was, for the Allied armies, a very important one. Where ever war was unleashed, infrastructure such as docks and landing facilities were high on the list of targets. Thus, as armies moved forward in need of a constant supply of materials, getting that support to the front-line Troops, without any docks, was one of the greatest hurdles to success for armies waging war on foreign soil.

Another equally pressing problem was the landing of troops on open beaches. Traditional landing vehicles, with their forward access, were very vulnerable when soldiers first left the vehicle directly into the combat zone, providing of course, the craft ever got to the beach. Sandbanks, hidden currents and war debris made the lumbering conventional landing craft far from an ideal tool for the success of an amphibious assault. Successful amphibious assaults would be essential for victory in both the European and Pacific Theatres of World War II. To come up with a solution, the American Government created an organisation aptly entitled the Office of Scientific Research and Development, or O.S.R.D. for short. With radical problems needing equally radical answers, engineers and scientists were absorbed into the O.S.R.D. from all levels of both military and civilian occupations. To tackle what would seem a virtually impossible equation, (a vehicle that could carry both men and supplies on land and water), O.S.R.D. engaged the expertise of three highly qualified individuals to come up with such a solution. There was the gifted engineer Frank W. Spear and one of their own employees, Palmer Cosslet Putnam, had already had success with a project for a vehicle to combat landings in snow and heavy mud. This led to another brilliant semi amphibious vehicle the Weasel. The third candidate was, on the surface, a rather odd choice but, as things worked out, an even more inspired one. Rod Stevens was a gifted designer of ocean-going yachts. His company, Sparkman and Stevens, designed numerous award-winning vessels including the 1937 Ranger, winner of several international events for the United States. The design of this new craft, to solve military problems that seemed virtually unsolvable, was to be one of his greatest achievements.

At this moment in our story it would seem most suitable for me to review those factors concerning the origins behind the vehicles' legendary title of D.U.K.W. Its pedigree was the GMC 6 by 6 standard military truck, the well-tried workhorse of the US army transport division. The GMC symbol for this vehicle was CCKW ( C=1941 K=Conventional K= front wheel drive W= two rear drive axles). Therefore, using GMCs standard system code names for its projects, this new craft became D-1942 U-utility (amphibious) K-front wheeled drive W-Two rear driving axles = D.U.K.W.

Putnam and Stevens wasted no time in designing and building a prototype vehicle. A mockup was constructed in the April of 1942, and 38 days later the first pilot model was rolled out. Support for the D.U.K.W. from the armed forces was lukewarm, with many top Generals doubtful as to its suitability. There were various demonstrations of the vehicles potential and three more pilot models were finished. Finally, the army decided they would order 2,000 vehicles following a very successful demonstration, however, further evaluations proved less able to circumvent the conventional thinking of the American Top Brass. The 2,000 D.U.K.W.s, new and unused were put into storage with a plan to eventually mothball them until the end of the war. It looked as if the fate of Stevens' greatest achievement was signed and sealed.

A combination of two events now played a significant contribution in the D.U.K.W.'s chequered birth. The O.S.R.D. organisation mounted one last demonstration to try and show the military top brass the full potential of the amphibian. They chose the small east coast town of Provincetown, Massachusetts. Stevens and Putnam attended the trials taking with them two prototype vehicles. Every possible effort was made to make the trial conditions as realistic as possible. Four days before the event, conditions in the designated area suddenly deteriorated with winds blowing at 60 MPH causing huge breaking surf and driving rain. Off shore a Coast Guard Patrol boat ran into difficulties. The vessel struck a sandbank over a quarter of a mile from the shore and due to the extreme conditions, the crew were unable either to use their onboard rescue equipment or to swim to safety. The Coast Guard assembled surf boats and breeches buoys on the beach in an attempt to mount a rescue operation from the shore. Again, this proved unworkable. It was at that point the Coast Guard commander requested help from the O.S.R.D team.

From their base, a mile or so from this developing incident, the two prototype D.U.K.W.s were driven out, one of them crewed by Stephens and Putnam. What followed laid the foundations of a rescue service some eight years later in a town far from that small community of Provincetown. One of the two D.U.K.W.s was left on the shore as back up, while the one crewed by Putnam, and Stephens, accompanied by a Coast Guard officer, plunged into the tide. Rolling and pitching the vehicle's GMC 6-cylinder engine battled against the massive waves.

Many times the onlookers on the beach saw the vessel disappear from sight only to emerge again, water pouring from its decks and bilge pumps. Stephens, with great skill, guided his creation to the Coast guard vessel, which was near to breaking up. The crew were exhausted from their ordeal, all hope of being rescued fading as rapidly as the boat beneath them. Then the D.U.K.W. appeared alongside with only minutes to spare and took all 7 members of the crew off and returned them safely to the beach. Altogether, the amphibian had taken less than half an hour to execute this rescue. As for the Coast Guard vessel Rose, it was literally smashed to pieces, never to be seen again!

The D.U.K.W.'s credentials as a revolutionary and highly effective military vehicle were now assured, though within a very short time it was not for that talent that the future fame of the vehicle was to unveil. The D.U.K.W.'s exploit off the Provincetown beach did not go unnoticed by the press who were covering the story.

A local newspaper reporter was on the beach watching the incident unfold. He made sure that his story got to the major papers who were hungry for copy to give their readers tales to feed a wartime appetite for good news. The headlines read....

## "AT CAPE COD AN ARMY TRUCK WENT TO SEA AND RESCUED THE CREW FROM A STRANDED NAVAL VESSEL".

This publication found its way on to the desk of Secretary for War Stimson, who took it into the next meeting with the US president Franklin D Roosevelt. It was from that moment on, the D.U.K.W. had a powerful friend and champion in the White House.

Further tests were hurriedly arranged. This time they were well attended and the potential of this new revolutionary amphibious vehicle was finally recognised. Both Putnam and Stephens were to remain very much involved in the D.U.K.W. programme, and were to see it become one of the most successful inventions of the second World War; but as we shall see, for some, that was only the beginning of the story!

Artwork: Author

**D.U.K.W. Production Figures**

(From chassis No. 353 total production; 21,147)

**Production:**

The General Motors Yellow Truck and Coach Plant At Pontiac, Michigan, USA.

Countries supplied:

- Britain: 2,000 units (lend/lease scheme)
- Canada: 800 units
- Russia: 586 units
- Australia:535 units

IN SICILY NO LESS THAN 90% of all supplies came in by D.U.K.W. on the vital second and third days of the Allied invasion of Italy. In Normandy, during the opening phase of the \D-Day landings, no less than 40% of all over beach supplies were D.U.K.W.-borne for more than four months.

It is an observable fact that a stone dropped into a pool causes ripples outwards far beyond the point of its impact. So it was with the story of the birth of the D.U.K.W. at the small hamlet of Provincetown, Massachusetts, New England. 3,000 miles across the Atlantic those ripples were to be felt seven years later, on the North West Lancashire coastline.

An ex-French Army D.U.K.W. after being mothballed since WWII
it stands at Seaforth dock heading for Doxey
Thompson and Doxey Workshops"

# CHAPTER THREE

# AGELESS HEROES

The small seaside town of Southport, which in the time of this story was in Lancashire, was relocated after the boundary changes, into Sefton MBC, Merseyside. It lies on the North-West coast of England, besides the Irish Sea. Our small seaside town is situated between the mouths of the Mersey River and the River Ribble 18 miles North-West of Liverpool.

In the 1940s this Victorian maritime township was aptly Nicknamed "England's Seaside Garden City". By the end of that era in 1901 the town's population was a mere 48,000 but by 2001 this had increased considerably to over 90,000 inhabitants.

The journey of the D.U.K.W. from its homeland in the United States really began when in 1925 Southport's lifeboat station, standing on the newly finished Esplanade, closed its doors for the last time, bringing to an end an institution that had served that community faithfully since 1786. This building was to stand redundant for many years until in December 1988 the Southport Inshore Rescue Trust would house their inflatable craft in the same building.

The Southport lifeboat, The John Harling, was the last RNLI to see active service off this coast. The John Harling had a record of 20 years' service prior to her retirement, and the vessels record of gallant rescues included the saving on some 63 individuals from the 13 wrecks she attended. But the combined forces of nature and man had influenced irreversibly this area of England's coastlines. These changes to the natural order, can be traced directly to human activity included the buildup of sand that began to fill Southport's South channel. This man-made change was a direct result of the extension of the Ribble Channel Revetment walls, built after the passing of the 1883 Ribble Navigation Bill. The dumping of sand and mud from the River Mersey, during the increased levels of dredging, was an added factor. Another factor was the diversion of the Crossens channel from the South Channel to the Pinfold Channel and land reclamation between Southport and Hesketh Bank, all manmade interventions to the nature of the coastline which stopped fresh water scouring the Channel of sand brought in by the tide.

These changes to the nature of the coastline affected every aspect of maritime life in the area. The fishing and shrimping industries after the 1920s declined rapidly, a decline which continues even to the present day. The end came too for the era of passenger steamships in the area, the end to Southport being a true port. The ships, operating from the end of Southport pier were both paddle and screw powered, and worked along the coast joining Southport to the Isle of Man, New Brighton, Llandudno, Bangor, Lytham, Preston, St. Annes and Blackpool. This service began in the summer of 1894, but in the August of 1923 the vessels PS Bickerstaffe and the Ribble Queen (owned by the Blackpool Passenger Co and the Ribble Passenger Transport Co) were the last ships to depart from the pier, the sand's incursion severing finally Southport's long link with the sea and sealing, probably for ever, the town's history as a port.

**Life-Boat J Harling  (Sefton Libraries)**
**COXSWAIN: Richard Robinson**

The John Harling, Southport's last life-boat (1904-1925).
**FACTFILE**
LENGTH: 43 feet BEAM: 13 feet
TYPE: Watson Pulling Boat
POWER: Sail and/or 12 oars DETAILS:
Water ballast tanks/drop keel made of bronze. BUILDERS:
Thames Ironworks Co.

Towards the end of the John Harling's service the silting up of the coastline meant that the lifeboat could only be launched two hours in every twenty-four. Eventually, orders came in 1924 from the local RNLI committee, to withdraw her from active service.

She was sold to the owners of the Marine Lake for £100.00. She ended her once heroic days as a launch, transporting visitors around the lake! A sad end to the Southport Lifeboat Service.

The Wreck Chrysopolis of Genoa  (Sefton Libraries)

The 2,931 ton Italian ship Chrysopolis of Genoa. 20th February 1918 she was the 10th wreck to which the John Harling was called. She was on transit to Liverpool from Genoa with a cargo of copper ore. She hit a huge natural obstacle called the Horsebank in thick fog. Later, despite efforts to save the ship, she then drifted further finally becoming stranded on Angry Brow before finishing up on Spencers' and became a total wreck.

The Wreck Chrysopolis of Genoa  (Sefton Libraries)

# CHAPTER FOUR

# THE FIRST PERIOD (1947 – 1953)

From the meetings of the St Annes Parks and Cemeteries Committee.

Minute No. 834, May 1947. Application by Edward P. Eden of 63 Roseacre, Blackpool for permission to operate an amphibious vehicle for pleasure trips in the season 1947

Minute No. 1073, June 1947. Granted the application by Mr Eden and Mr J G Routledge to operate three amphibious vehicles to the North side of the beach road for pleasure trips.

Also….

From the minutes of the Southport Corporation Publicity and Attractions Committee.

No. 3393, July 1947. "The committee authorised for a trial trip in a 'duck' and subject to this trial proving satisfactory, for the Night and Day Garage Service Liverpool, to have the right to operate a service of 'ducks' from a point immediately north of the pier for the remainder of the present, ie until the 28th September 1947, inclusive, at a fee of £30, subject to all operational details being approved by this committee and to an agreement to be prepared by the Town Clerk."

The war years would still have been fresh in the memory of people living in Britain when these lines were entered into the rather official pages of Southport and St Annes archives, however, as one can read, the minds of some individuals were turning to the future, especially the rebirth of regular recreational activities for the working population of this austerity stricken, post war country. There were many opportunities to be exploited in this period, not the least of which was the rebirth of a British Institution which had been well and truly flattened during the war years, the British Summer seaside holiday! The once prosperous, traditional seaside towns up and down the country's coastline had suffered badly during the war years. Now was the time to encourage people to return, but it would not be easy. In those bleak days of the late 1940s, money was scarce, and rivalry between towns, for what they could offer the public must have been uppermost in the minds of their governing bodies. New ideas were urgently needed. As we can see Southport and St Annes were by no means alone in this dilemma, traditional rivals were also drawing up their future plans to attract new visitors.

A year earlier in 1946, a certain Mr John Routledge had approached Blackpool Corporation with an ambitious plan involving the use of D.U.K.W.s as a tourist attraction, a plan far in advance of those later adopted by Blackpool's close rivals. Mr Routledge's idea was to link Blackpool with its close neighbours St Annes and Southport using D.U.K.W. tours! This was indeed ambitious (or maybe just amphibious) plans, especially when you consider the implications of such natural hazards as the currents in the Ribble Estuary, the sandbanks littering the coastline, the very changeable weather conditions.

Not to mention the somewhat less than luxury conditions aboard an open D.U.K.W.! It would appear that the Chief Constable of Blackpool had similar misgivings and the application was rejected!

New Brighton D. U. K. W. (Reflections photo archive)

One of Blackpool, Southport and St Annes' very progressive Merseyside seaside holiday towns stole the march on its rivals when it came to the use of ex-military amphibious vehicles as a holiday attraction. Again with the involvement of Mr John Routledge, New Brighton's golden beaches in 1946 were the first to host a new ride into the sea, and very popular they proved too. The New Brighton venture was a partnership between John Routledge and Mr Cliff Street of Wallasey. The two men operated an ex-US army D.U.K.W. and an ex-British army six and a half-ton Terrapin six wheeled amphibian during the 1946 summer season. During this period the idea to colour the vehicles in a red and cream livery was invented, as this would make them more visible when at sea. This idea was to have interesting implications when applied to other ventures in other towns but more on that later.

I must mention here a little bit more about Mr Cliff Street. Mr Street made eleven escapes from German prisoner of war camps during WW II! He volunteered for the RAF as a pilot. Although at first rejected due to his age, he finally succeeded in becoming a navigator at the rank of Warrant Officer. His Halifax bomber was shot down over Düsseldorf in 1942, and after escaping from various camps he ended up in the infamous Stalag 344. He escaped twice after learning to speak German and forging identity papers which even fooled the Gestapo. The privations he suffered during these years, however, affected his future health. I could only find evidence that the New Brighton venture lasted the one season. Indeed I could find no record of Mr Street after 1949, which leads me to wonder as to what befell him. John Routledge, however, used the New Brighton experience to develop amphibious activities in Southport and St Annes. If Cliff Street was a colourful example of a post war entrepreneur, John Routledge's story is in a league of its own! Before we delve a little deeper into that, there were more amphibious activities further up the NW coast at St Annes. John Routledge's name again is associated with another D.U.K.W. based enterprise. This time he was in partnership with an Edward P Eden from Blackpool. They were given permission in 1947, by the St Annes' Parks and Cemeteries committee, to mount an operation on the foreshore of St Annes. Their base was to be south of Squires Gate holiday camp and north of Beach Road.

Three amphibious D.U.K.W.s were employed by Eden and Routledge in the first season, one for the transportation of passengers, one as a backup and the third under maintenance. Early in 1948 Edward Eden renewed his agreement with St Annes local authority. That season, however, was not a profitable one for the enterprise being plagued with adverse weather conditions throughout much of the summer months. In the autumn of 1948 Mr Eden was granted a reduction in the concession terms to help compensate for revenue losses that season. Two of the St Annes' D.U.K.W.s were back on the beach for the 1949 season for the last time. Again a combination of weather and mechanical problems continued to plague the venture. The two partners decided to cut their losses and sold the business.

The red and yellow D.U.K.W.s never returned to the golden beaches of St Annes.

Returning briefly to the meeting of the Southport Publicity and Attractions committee, of July 1947, which gave the go ahead to Mr John Routledge of Liverpool to operate during the 1947/48 season, the Liverpool based salvage specialist and business expert set about purchasing vehicles to run the new passenger service. He had plenty of experience to fall back on. Together with his son, Phil, under the name of J. Routledge and Sons (Liverpool), many ex-military surplus vehicles were purchased for use by the company itself or for resale and export. This experience went back indeed to post WW II when heavy, ex-military vehicles played an important role in the demolition business, the removing of blitzed buildings in Manchester and Liverpool as well as the recovery and disposal of wrecked ships in Liverpool docks.

The D.U.K.W.s that first appeared on Southport's beaches were purchased at military surplus sales in Sevenoaks, Doncaster and Sheffield. That distinctive red and yellow colour scheme was again adopted as the livery for those involved in beach operations. (It also just happened that Southport buses also sported the same colour scheme, which was a practice going back into the mist of automotive time.) Bus-style wooden benches were added inside some D.U.K.W.s for the comfort of passengers.

However the cargo compartment bows, used to support the military cargo tarpaulin cover, were removed, the D.U.K.W.s were left open, and the tarpaulin itself discarded. The removal of the unique but somewhat complicated tyre inflation system does not appear to have been a policy with the Routledge D.U.K.W.s since the firm probably had the mechanical expertise to maintain them. This was not the case with other private operators who found their retention both expensive and unnecessary. The tyre inflation system allowed the D.U.K.W. driver to select the vehicle's tyre pressure to suit the conditions encountered, and the pressure could then be raised or lowered from the cab without the D.U.K.W. needing to stop, a feature automotive technology ahead of its time. With the main use of the Routledge D.U.K.W.s being salvage work in and around the docks, the device may indeed have been very useful. J. Routledge and Sons of Liverpool, as mentioned, carried out many marine operations in the Northwest. Two of these certainly deserve a mention. Both were related by J. Routledge's grandson Rob and deserve further research if you are a maritime history enthusiast.

Empress of Canada

In 1953 the Cunard liner Empress of Canada slid into the Gladstone Dock to undergo a much needed refit but on the night of 25th January 1953 the vessel was engulfed by a horrific fire. In a vain attempt to control the huge blaze, fighters poured thousands of gallons of water into the ship's hull. The weight of this caused the Empress to slowly roll over onto her side crushing masts and funnels against the dock side, an event mirroring a previous similar tragedy involving the French liner Normandie which also caught fire in New York harbour before capsizing. The French salvage company Comax who were employed to salvage the Empress called on the diving experience of Phil Routledge, gained in the grey waters of the Liverpool dockyards. The task of raising the stricken Empress was to test even the well practiced diving skills of engineer Phil Routledge. Wearing heavy conventional diving equipment, complete with huge helmet, weighed belt and boots, for nearly a year he plunged into the murky depths of Gladstone dock. Air was pumped into his helmet through a lengthy, heavy rubber air tube which gave him the ability to work beneath the liner for several, exhausting hours at a time. The salvage plan required several heavy steel cables to be passed under the ship's partly upturned hull. These were then attached to a line of steam powered winches positioned in line along the length of the quayside. To accomplish this plan Phil had to force a channel through the deep mud on the bed of the dock, using only a fire hose! A rope attached to the steel cable was threaded through the gap and the cable followed, All this had to be accomplished before the mud could fill up the passage. So much for the technology of 1953!

Empress of Canada

Finally, as the year ended the preparations were completed and the task of raising the vessel began.

All the ships' holds were sealed shut and air pumped into the hull. The huge steam winches took the strain and within a very short time the badly damaged Empress of Canada rolled back upright. She was too badly damaged to save, as had been hoped, the scrap yard became her last port of call. Phil was given the ship's bell by its captain to remember his hours beneath his ship.

**Phil Routledge with original dive helmet which he wore while diving under the Empress of Canada.**

Within a few months, the Routledge company could be found only 15 miles away, on Southport's bright and sunny beach. The salvage problem they encountered there, however, did not really compare with the one involving the old Empress.

RECORDS: of the Southport Publicity and Attractions committee. October 1947.

"That a tender be invited for the right to operate a service of DUCKS on the foreshore, from a point immediately north of the pier. From the 25th March 1948 to 3rd October 1948. *Tender awarded to Mr J. Rankin for the amount of £750*

D U K W s are a Popular Attraction for Sea Cruises off Southport Shore.

### Routledge Duck Southport

As the first season of the Routledge's Southport D.U.K.W. venture came to an end, changes were already in the pipeline. The moderate success of this unusual leisure venture had not gone unnoticed by certain officers of the Publicity and Attractions committee. Reading the minutes of their committee meetings you can quickly notice that the price of the tender rose from just £30 in 1947 to £750 in 1948! A considerable mark-up in a post war, austerity strapped Britain. At this point, no doubt influenced by this considerable rise in costs, the firm decided to withdraw and concentrate on their very successful demolition and salvage business. J. Routledge & Sons is still very much in business even to this day. Eventually, the Duck tender was awarded to Ex RNR Lieutenant Joseph Rankin.

After a very active career serving with the Royal Navy in the Mediterranean, North Africa and Greece, in 1947 Joseph Rankin was discharged after two years extra voluntary service after WW II. At the same time of his discharge from the navy, Joe had a number of close friends living in the North-West. One of these was a fellow naval officer he served with in his last years in the navy. Aware of Rankin's imminent naval retirement, this colleague contacted him on the subject of the Southport

Corporation's advert for the D.U.K.W. tender. Both men had worked extensively on Royal Navy D.U.K.W.s, Consequently, Joe Rankin was awarded the contract to begin operating the amphibians for leisure purposes in the 1948 summer season.

On arriving back in the town, the now ex naval officer found he had a lot to do to be ready for that season, especially as he did not actually own even one single vehicle! This did not prove to be any serious problem as the market was flooded with surplus military equipment. The new Labour government was slashing defence spending and the size of the armed services. Spare parts were also readily available, not to mention a nearly endless supply of ex-military mechanics who could maintain the D.U.K.W. fleet. A very positive situation for such a new venture. Quickly,a small but very skilled team was recruited and they formed the basis of the company's workforce for the next few years.

**1950 Beach Buses:**
**Beach scene north of Southport pier. A red and white Ex-army Bedford QL bus parked in the foreground. A special body and wooden seats for added comfort! Two of Rankin's ducks loading passengers behind**

In less than eight months Joe had enough of the sea going veterans to open for business in the April of 1948.He purchased land on the edge of the town in order to build sheds and workshops to house his fleet and to maintain them for the demands of both the public and the sea.

Most of the early two and a half ton vehicles Rankin bought were the Mark 1

D.U.K.W, known for its completely flat window screen and its spare tyre on the right-hand side at the rear deck. These vehicles were purchased from military surplus equipment sales up and down the country.

Various equipment and cosmetic changes were introduced before any of the amphibians embarked on a new career of carrying the general public out to sea on joyrides.

Their new owners soon realised their war veterans would have to be made as functional as possible. On arrival, engines were stripped out and reconditioned. The exhaust outlet, situated just beneath the driver's window, was redirected up a single improvised funnel in order to direct the fumes away from the passengers. Rankin's mechanics next removed some of the D.U.K.W.s standard fittings, which were considered unsuitable for their day to day use as leisure vehicles. These included the canvass hoods, the support hoops, spare tyres, some of the instrumentation, not to mention that automatic tyre inflation system. As the vehicles were often parked outside in compounds, it became the policy to remove the entire window screen unit to avoid acts of vandalism.

This practical improvisation, however, proved to be the source of another unforeseen problem for the vehicle's driver, when the D.U.K.W. was at sea in even small wave conditions. All ducks were fitted with a steel surf board attached to the forward front deck. In the first few months of Leisure operations it was soon discovered that the standard surf board did not deflect enough spray from the driver's compartment and to make matters worse it often reached the passengers! This practice of getting a good soaking did not exactly encourage paying customers to return for a second trip or to recommend the D.U.K.W. trip to family and friends. This problem was solved, however, by the Rankin team who came up with an extended plywood surfboard, longer and deeper than the original, which protected both driver and passengers (well, most of the time!) This was later strengthened with fiberglass.

Positioned at the rear of even the earliest ducks and to all marks thereafter, was a piece of equipment considered by the duck's inventors to be one of its most important assets. This was a very powerful Gar Wood drum winch. The winch had the ability to pull weights in access of 10,000 pounds. It derived its power from the D.U.K.W's engine through a power take off and could be controlled directly from the driver's compartment. An "A" frame could be fitted and, in conjunction with the drum winch, objects up to two and a half tons in weight, could be lifted and moved with ease. To remain an effective tool, these winches needed regular attention. This expenditure presented a dilemma, as each vehicle in the fleet was assigned a certain budget to keep costs down.

There was some debate on the case of stripping out the winches and even reselling them to help with expenses. Joe Rankin, with his Navy experience, decided against such a move. He had witnessed in the navy situations where duck crews literally winched their vehicles out of trouble.

This technique, used by Allied military duck crews, had proved invaluable time and time again. If a D.U.K.W. managed to get itself stuck in deep mud or sand, when even its powerful six-wheel drive could not get her out, the crew would then turn to the winch and the substantial sea anchor. A solid surface was investigated, even if some distance from the amphibian. The winch cable was then run out and the anchor sunk into the supporting surface. Next, power from the engine engaged the winch and slowly but surely the duck could winch itself out of trouble provided the winch cable held!

With this in mind, Rankin retained all the winches on his fleet of amphibious vehicles. A wise move on his part as the," winch myself free" technique, together with a multitude of other uses, would keep his duck crew's winching skills busy in the years to come!

*1948 February. Minutes of the meeting of the Southport Publicity and Attractions committee." That the application of Mr. Joseph Rankin to park his amphibious craft, at his own risk,in the Bathing Lake car park during the summer season, be granted.*

To drive the petrol guzzling, slow moving amphibious vehicles from their base at the north end of town to the operating area by the pier, was certainly time consuming. In the weekend rush hours, also a little dangerous due to the restricted view a driver has of both road and smaller vehicles. (Pretty well all vehicles in the 1940s and 50s were smaller than the D.U.K.W. with the exception of some commercial vehicles). Apparently following a duck with its steering still connected to the rudder was a little unsettling for following drivers. Constant exposure to sun, sea and sand, over the summer months, coupled with only basic maintenance, did not help the road reliability of some of the amphibians in Joe's fleet. The less the vehicles travelled on the road the better. This cooperation with the Southport Corporation Publicity and Attractions department, helped to solve this problem.

When the D.U.K.W.s first took up their stations on the Esplanade in the early months of 1948, they faced a very different coastline than that of today. From the area North of the pier extending several miles towards Banks and South towards Formby Point lay the flat golden sands of the North- West coastline.

*1948/September. Minutes of the Southport Publicity and Attractions Committee.* These letters show the planning for the next 12 months, as Southport began to formulate a programme for the 48/49 season. Joseph Rankin's D.U.K.W. business was now well established and there were plans to expand both in vehicle numbers and personnel. In reply to Joe's request, the committee offered him a concession to either operate four ducks at Southport and two at Ainsdale for a cool £800 or six ducks at Southport and two at Ainsdale for £1,000.The 1949 season was to also include a certain ironic event in so much as J.H. Lawson Booth published his second book on the local Lifeboat service, "A History of Southport Lifeboats".

Thus by sheer coincidence Southport Corporation decided to experiment with a new rescue service, in an attempt to combat the rising number of life threatening incidents occurring along the shoreline from the Ribble to the Mersey. This new service would have the WW II Amphibian as its main rescue vehicle. Negotiations with Rankin were concluded during 1949 when the Committee agreed a sum of £1,000 for the use of two vehicles with crews the following year. This fee was offset against that charged by the Attractions committee for the duck business. The appearance of the WW II amphibious vehicle in April 1950, in its role as a rescue vehicle, meant that, for the first time since the withdrawal of the lifeboat John Harling in 1925, the coast had a regular rescue service. Before that day, when the first grey painted D.U.K.W. rumbled onto the beach manned by Lifeguards, the nearest vessels capable of saving lives were the lifeboats of New Brighton and Lytham.

In the earliest days of the new D.U.K.W. rescue service, no official records have survived the rigours of time, if indeed there were any in the first place. Luckily, there is a more unusual and perhaps more accurate account of the activities of the amphibious rescue service off the Southport, Birkdale, Ainsdale and Formby beaches. This record took the form of three scrapbooks in which Joe Rankin collected articles from the Southport Visiter, Guardian and other national papers. These articles covered the period from 1949 to the late 1950s and form a unique picture of the pioneering work in a community service which was eventually to last for nearly five decades and save at a conservative estimate, the lives of over 600 men, women and children. The author was privileged to have access to this record before Mr. Rankin's recent death.

## 1948 (June)

(VISITER): The very first day of the Ainsdale summer season D.U.K.W. carrying 12 passengers diverted to a leaking dingy owned by a 22year old Aintree man. The owner's brother tried to swim to the shore but suffered exhaustion.

**SEPTEMBER:** A shrimping cart, horse and owner caught in quick-sands. Rescue carried out by Rankin, all saved and cart salvaged.

**NOVEMBER:** 9 people stranded on the foreshore surrounded by incoming tide, they were picked up by the Southport D.U.K.W..

**DECEMBER:** Fishing party marooned when D.U.K.W. engine failed!9 fishermen spent 12 hours (instead of 5) onboard. Battery ran down and so did the bilge pump. All bailing was done by hand. D.U.K.W. came to rest on a sandbank, before striking an underwater object in the dark. A couple of minor injuries sustained. The police guide the D.U.K.W. back using the headlights of police cars from the Marine drive.

Joe Rankin Shrimping D.U.K.W.

Powered by a Perkins 6 cylinder diesel engine this D.U.K.W. was outfitted in 1983 in an attempt to recreate the old duck pleasure trip market.

1983. SUMMER. D.U.K.W. SEA WOLF. PRIVATE OWNER. BEDFORD ENGINE CONVERSION. (DIESEL) 'A' FRAME TRAWL NET EXPERIMENT. FOR GENERAL FISHING AND SHRIMPING.

### 1949 (April)

(SOUTHPORT GUARDIAN) April: a car trapped by incoming tide towed to safety by a D.U.K.W. driven by Rankin.

10th AUGUST: A beach bus full of passengers became stuck in soft sand and an incoming tide. The passengers, some carrying older members of the public, abandon the bus to lighten the weight. Two of Rankin's D.U.K.W.s help in the recovery of the bus which eventually arrives with all passengers but half an hour late.

**29<sup>th</sup> AUGUST: a breakdown lorry on a mission to recover**

A car became bogged down in mud at Ainsdale, then itself gets into trouble! The car was already under 4 feet of water when the lorry arrived. Sea water then engulfed the lorry's engine. Two D.U.K.W.s working north of the pier arrive on the scene. The car has totally submerged and only the lorry's crane can be seen above the surface. Steel hawsers part of the amphibians equipment Rankin ordered retained, were fastened to each vehicle. They were both winched free of sand and sea but badly damaged.

Still from the film 'Lancashire Coast'

**26<sup>th</sup> October (Southport Guardian). The 40foot launch**

Dolphin on route from Dublin to Liverpool suffered engine trouble in a gale and heavy seas. With a crew of 4 she tied up at the pier. A young crew member master Charles Hampton, jumped from the deck with a line. He broke his leg on landing. The boat was later driven on to a sandbank at Crossens where the rest of the crew were taken off by D.U.K.W..

## OCTOBER to NOVEMBER BEACH CONCESSION GAIN GRANTED

**TO j. Rankin. for the sum of £1,000.**

**1950 Season. Duck Tours begin.**

Margaret James was eight or nine when she rode a D.U.K.W. in the 60s. She described the experience as very bumpy as the D.U.K.W. crashed through the waves!

**The 12 named D.U.K.W.s used in the 1950 Summer season were....**

- Black Jack
- Commando
- Donald Duck
- Jane
- Moby Dick
- Long John Silver
- Monkey Joe
- Silver King
- Dragon fly
- Swordfish
- Albatross
- Snow White
- Tombola

Rankin's agreement with the Publicity and Attractions department to allow him to accommodate fishing trips was also extended to the use of the vehicles for shrimping and cockling activities.

These industries were long established on the North west coastline as the conditions were just right to allow this delicacy to flourish, Morecambe Bay perhaps being the most prolific and long-lasting shrimping ground in the area, even to this day.

(The rate for charging for passengers was also fixed at 9d for a child and 1/- for an adult.)

At the beginning of the 1950s the use of the D.U.K.W. to harvest shell fish, became a serious proposition.

After the chaos of the war years, local shrimps and cockles were in very good supply and the market price for them began to climb as demand increased.

The economic revival gathered pace. North Western seaside towns such as New Brighton, Blackpool, Lytham, Lytham St.Annes ,Morecambe and of course Southport itself were some of the first small towns to benefit from this upturn. The increase in the popularity of seafood delicacies then began to spread inland and across the Pennines from Lancashire and into Yorkshire.

The shrimping season of September to December/January could not have been more convenient for the D.U.K.W. owners as it dovetailed nicely into the end of the tourist season which normally would have meant the end of any income supply. Joe Rankin would then normally lay off most of his staff.

Shortly after Rankin returned to Southport he met up with a local engineer and part time shrimper Dermot (Dave) Bunting an employee of the Southport engineering company of Brockhouse Engineering. Bunting's innovations in the art of catching the local Brown shrimp did not exactly make him a star in the eyes of the local traditional horse and cart shrimpers.

Rankin DUKW with on board shrimp treatment ovens (G. Rimmer)

A DUKW (PN-14) used as a shrimping vehicle 1960

Shrimper Peter Chorley and his amphibious ford jeep 1950

**Author Shrimping Photos**

Bunting experimented using mechanical horsepower instead of the hoofed variety! As an ex-army mechanic he was only too aware of the huge influx of cheap ex-military vehicles flooding into the civilian market which helped lower prices. He invested in a few 4wheel drive lorries and began using them for shrimping. There is no doubt there were nodding heads at this attempt to break the century long tradition of using horse and cart, especially when one of Buntings' vehicles broke down in the tide. The sea engulfed the vehicle which had to be recovered by a D.U.K.W. Within 48 hours, the lorry was back in action gathering a new haul of shrimps. This innovation was gradually adopted by more and more local fishermen. The tractor and later the huge rig gradually forced the cart and the faithful shrimper's horse into retirement. By the middle of the 1970s, they had become only a memory.

Spurred on no doubt by the already mentioned increasing lucrative shellfish industry, Rankin diverted some of his older D.U.K.W.s to his new shell fish enterprise. A pound of shrimps in 1952/53 could fetch 2/- (or around £15 in todays money)

The D.U.K.W. in its new role as a fishing vehicle, however, had mixed fortunes. Each vehicle had a crew of 5, a driver and 4 men working the nets. The vehicles worked in pairs just in case there were any mechanical problems as most of them, by then, were well over the age that their designers had envisaged they would be in use!

Once a D.U.K.W. arrived in a shrimping area, 3 to 4 nets were deployed from a wooden platform built onto the rear deck. Two other nets were also then attached to a long, heavy pole called a Boom each side of the vehicle on a tow rope some 20 feet long. Each net, called a Shank net (hence the shrimper is traditionally called a Shanker), was around 10 feet in length and cone shaped. The mouth of the net, as it is being dragged along in the shallow water of the incoming tide, is kept open by a strong iron frame and once the D.U.K.W. was in action the crew would work in half hour shifts. The nets would be hauled in one at a time and the contents emptied into stout wicker baskets.

Perhaps one of the advantages of working with a D.U.K.W. was the space it offered inside for the crew to work. In a cart the shrimper had very limited space in which to store his catch before the long journey home and the task of boiling the shrimps. Shrimpers had shrimp boiling facilities in their cottages where, once home, they would first boil the catch and then shell them ready for the market. All this took time and Joe soon realised not only was his vehicle much quicker at getting too and fro from the shrimping grounds, but that there was time and space to conduct an interesting experiment. During one season in the early 1950s, Joe Rankin fitted an oven into the cargo compartment on one of his vehicles. The idea of this was that the task of processing the shrimps could be further reduced by actually boiling them on board. The fact that the oven was situated just above the fuel lines did not appear to concern Joe too much! Attempts were also made to try and reduce the size of the D.U.K.W.s' crew. He devised a powered net device which could haul in the catch without the need for too many human hands. This diesel powered machine proved, at best, only just about equal to its human counterpart!

**DUCK CRASHES INTO HUT** (1950 July. Guardian}

"Several amphibious vehicles called D.U.K.W.s were parked behind the outdoor Sea Bathing lake at night. An intruder tampered with one vehicle and managed to start it. The vehicle demolished part of a corporation building!"

**COACH DRAGGED OUT.** (Visiter /August)) no less than 16 coaches got stuck on the beach this weekend in 1950. A duck vehicle was kept busy for several hours.

**SCHOONER BATTERED BY STORMS** (September) Various articles both in the Guardian and the Visiter between 16th and 18th September.

### NORTH-WEST RESORT LIKE BATTLFIELD AFTER GREAT GALE.

Lancashire Evening Post 18th/09/50. Several paragraphs with accounts of the HAPPY HARRY incident and the role of Southport's D. U. K. W.s in the salvage attempt of the vessel in very hazardous conditions.

FIRST TO BE EQUIPED WITH HEAVY DUTY LADDER.

DUKW No4 LATE 1950s (PHTO: BRAN CNETT)

**NOT SO HAPPY HARRY.** (Daily Telegraph) included an interview with Joe Rankin on his attempt to board the Irish vessel, in the middle of a huge storm.

All the articles carried stories on the role played by Joe and his men as they battled the storm aboard a D.U.K.W. in the sad tale of the wrecking of the Happy Harry. REPORT: Sunday 15th Sept 1950....

* The Irish schooner Happy Harry built in 1894 was driven into the Formby channel by a 75mph gale after her engine failed.

* The vessel was voyaging from county Wicklow (Ireland) to Garston docks with a mixed cargo.

The Crew abandon the Happy Harry, leaving the vessel to her fate.

* A D.U.K.W. vehicle belonging to Joseph Rankin and carrying three of his team is launched into the sea off Ainsdale.

The D.U.K.W. reaches the stricken vessel but crashes into the schooner's side! The salvage crew board with difficulty. Pump water from engine room. Fail to restart engine. Ship's anchors secure the ship, no longer drifting. 12.30 Monday morning. STORM BLOWING OUT. Salvage crew leave ship.

REPORT: Monday midnight; STORM RETURNS FROM ATLANTIC:

Happy Harry drags its anchors: salvage team fail to get back in time.

TUESDAY 5.30am H.H. crashes into Southport Pier! Considerable damage to the pier supports: fire brigade are called out and the crippled vessel is pumped full with several thousand gallons of water: further damage averted.

20th Sept. 1950 The battered Irish schooner Happy Harry by the pier. A Rankin DUKW in attendance! (Sefton Libraries))

Drill 6 holes in the hull of the
ill fated schooner Happy
Harry. Sticks of gelignite
were inserted (background)
In the first effort to blow the
wreck up.

**1951 (28.2.51) Southport Guardian. (Sefton Libraries)**

The Happy Harry is a total wreck and takes many months to dismantle. She is
eventually blown up and burnt.

## TIDE TRAPS SWIMMER WITH GREYHOUNDS.

SWIMMER SAVED FROM SEA PERIL (Visiter) A local swimmer Austin Neame
got trapped on a sandbank with his 3 Greyhounds. A number of vehicles attempted a
rescue but only a D.U.K.W. driven by Joe succeeded. The owner hung onto his pets as
the tide poured over them. Unluckily one of the animals was drowned. The owner
tried to defraud the insurance company by overstating the value of his pet!

8.8.51 (Guardian) (Visiter); YACHT SWAMPS A MILE OFFSHORE. 3 man crew of
the 30 foot motor yacht Permit on route to the Isle of Man in danger as the boat
swamped in heavy seas. D.U.K.W. dispatched to take the crew off but the tide proved
to be too aggressive. The New Brighton lifeboat completes the mission successfully.

## A New Sea Rescue Service

In the December of 1951 a sea bathing ban, brought in at the outbreak of the War, was finally lifted from the Southport, Birkdale, Ainsdale and Formby beaches. As a safety measure, D.U.K.W.s owned by Joseph Rankin were officially deployed on Southport and Ainsdale beaches to reintroduce a regular rescue service, the first since the end of the lifeboats in 1925. At this point in time, the Southport Publicity and Attractions department, did not actually purchase their own vehicles. Instead they subcontracted the job to the person best suited to organise and maintain the vehicles. In the early days of the service Rankin was contracted to have one D.U.K.W. at Ainsdale, a patrol duck at Southport and a reserve vehicle kept in the Outdoor Pool's car park.

SEA RESCUE From the Southport Visiter editorial of 8th December 1951, heralding a new era for the town and the safety of its beaches.

This service was to endure for nearly 5 decades with a conservative estimate of over 600 lives saved.

It was 1998 when the last D.U.K.W. was owned by Sefton M.B.C.

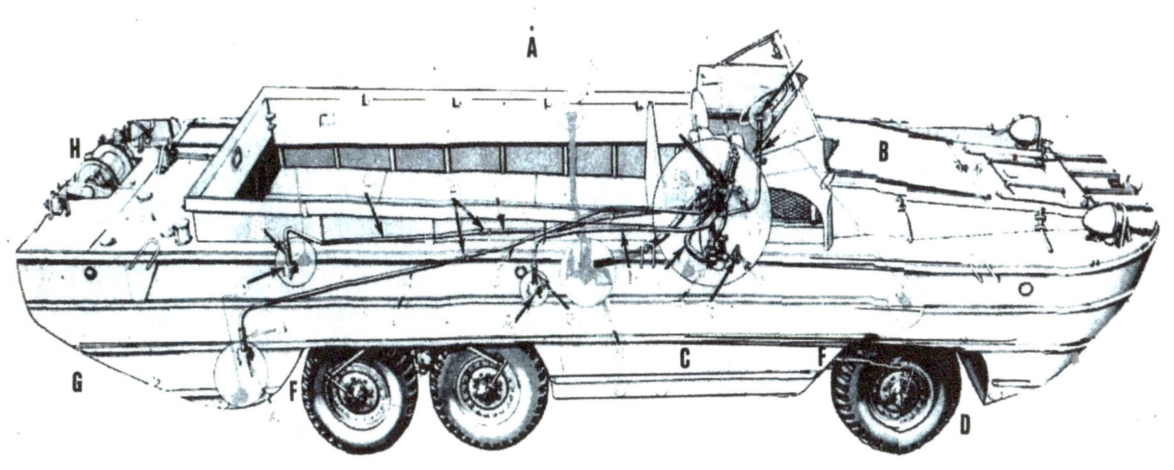


### JUST A FEW of the Mk2 D.U.K.W.s TECHNICAL POINTS

**A. Parts:** 85%: of the D.U.K.W.s parts were already in use before its invention. These parts were made for the D.U.K.W.s parent vehicle the General Motors CCKW-353 two and a half ton 6x6 truck.

**B. THE ENGINE:** Its design was nearly 10 years old when it was selected as the D.U.K.W.s' power plant. Estimated at least half a million engines already produced by 1942 by General Motors.

**C. BILGE PUMPS:** dual system detailed in the chapter The Second Period. The third part of this vital system was a hand operated pump usually carried by military vehicles on the forward hull.

Often disregarded by early civilian operators.

# The DUKW Drivers World

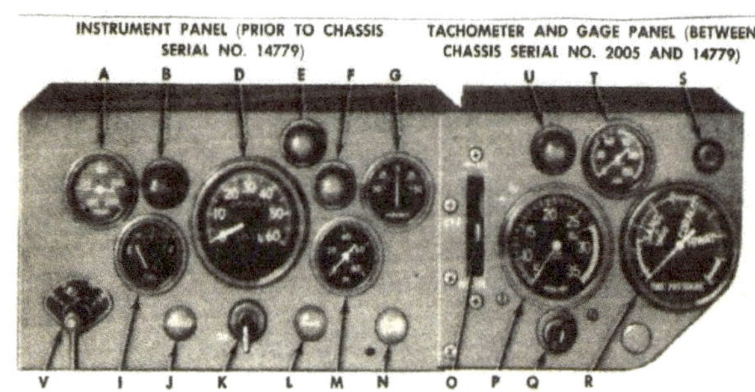


DUKW INSTRUMENT PANEL. NOT ALL THESE DEVICES WERE USED BY THE VEHICLES IN RANKINS/ SOUTHPORT/SEFTON AMPHIBIANS.

THE DRIVER'S VIEW FROM HIS CAB ABOARD THE DUKW. THERE WERE FEW COMFORTS IN HIS SPARTAN SURROUNDINGS. AHEAD THE SURF-BOARD IN RAISED POSITION. EVEN THE WINDOW WHIPERS HAVE BEEN REMOVED!!

DRIVERS OF RESCUE DUKWS OFTEN WERE RESPONSIBLE FOR THE EARLY DETECTION OF ANY PROBLEMS THEIR VEHICLES DEVELOPED.

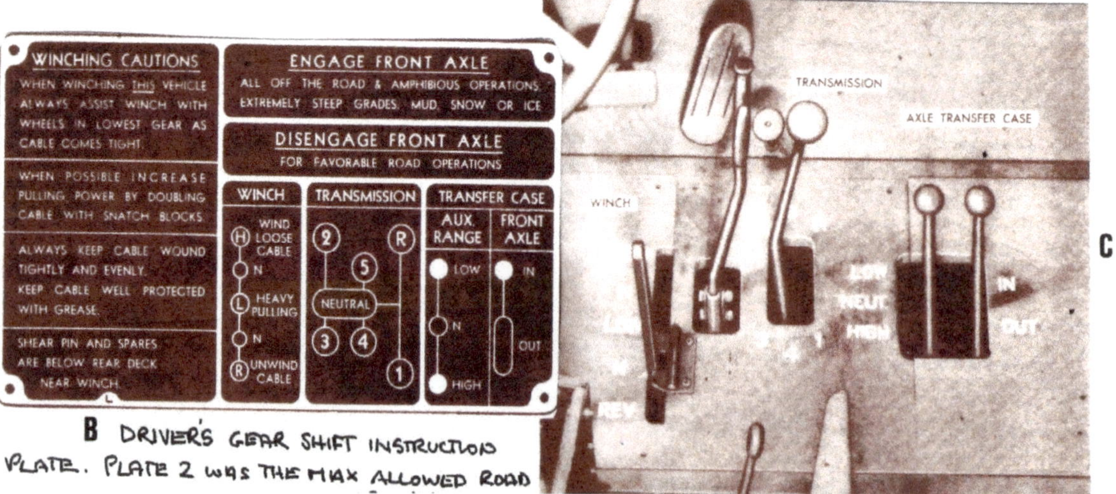


B DRIVER'S GEAR SHIFT INSTRUCTION PLATE. PLATE 2 WAS THE MAX ALLOWED ROAD

Inside the Cockpit of A D.U.K.W.

**D. TURNING CIRCLE:** The turning circle of a D.U.K.W. was 40 feet on land: The rudder was attached to the steering wheel unit. The D.U.K.W.'s front wheels could also be used to assist steering in water.

**E. ADDITIONAL DATA:** During production and operation there were over 800 modifications to the original design! 25 of these were of major significance to the development of the amphibian as an effective tool of the Allied armies.

**F. TYRE INFLATION SYSTEM:** an automotive invention well ahead of its time. This allowed the driver to select which tyre pressure he considered appropriate when the D.U.K.W. was in operational situations. This was operated from a switch in the driver's cab.

**G. REVOLUTIONARY DESIGN:** the designers of the O.S.R.D. unit took the main units of the GMC truck and wrapped them in a sheet metal boat shaped body. With the GMC truck being a well proved design, the millions of available parts were interchangeable with the D.U.K.W.

**H. GAR WOOD WORM DRIVEN HORIZONTAL WINCH:** this powerful tool which made the D.U.K.W. a formidable vehicle when it came to recovering other vehicles and indeed rescuing itself! It was a valued part of the ducks equipment both in its military and civilian careers.

**The Powerful Garwood Winch:
The first period 1947 to 1953**

# CHAPTER FIVE

# THE SECOND PERIOD (1953 TO 1973)

## The Great 1953 East Coast Flood Disaster

During the 31st January 1953 an exceptional mixture of bad weather conditions and the seasonal spring tides led to perhaps the worst natural disaster in Britain's post war history. On that day huge waves, many in excess of six metres in height and driven by 100mph winds, pounded the coastline of South- east England. A direct result of this, the sea defences were breached in over a thousand places. In a Britain, still facing great post Wartime austerity, the finance to keep up the repairs to such items of infrastructure, was very hard to find. Consequently, 307 people were killed within a few hours,46,000 livestock also lost their lives, 24,000 homes were destroyed and 160,000 acres of Britain's best farmland went under the sea.

Great Lincolnshire Flood, as it was to become aptly named, at a conservative estimate cost the country five Billion pounds in today's money.

The initial response by the emergency services to this flood disaster was, at best, chaotic. Typical, however, during events such as these, there were many individual acts of heroism from the ranks of the Police, Fire Services and the armed forces who struggled in horrendous conditions to save both people, animals and property. It was often the personal courage and endeavour of the ordinary citizen, however, that saved the situation from becoming much worse. Many owed their lives, their homes and indeed their whole communities to these unrecorded selfless actions.

Within just a few days of the great storm two red and cream Southport D.U.K.W.s trundled from their home base to travel the 130 miles to Mablethorpe, Lincolnshire. Joe Rankin had offered his services and those of his D.U.K.W. company within a few hours of the disaster. In those early days of the 1950s the British army was equipped with a substantial number of these vehicles but most were based abroad. Those in the UK were soon deployed, but the situation was growing increasingly serious. Joe Rankin wasted no more time and prepared his team and vehicles for the task ahead.

Joe Rankin drives one of his Southport's pleasure D.U.K.W.s through a battered and flooded street of a town in Lincolnshire.

On board the vehicle are local council officers and members of the emergency services. One concerned passenger, a fellow naval officer comrade of Rankins, none other than the Duke of Edinburgh who visited the area on numerous occasions to view the relief operation.

**1953 Britain's Prince Philip inspects flood damage
(permission Rexfeatures Ltd)**

With 32 year old Rankin at the wheel of the D.U.K.W. Dragonfly, the convoy of the two amphibians arrived in the midst of the post flood chaos. A second vehicle was driven by Joe's right hand man Hyton Steinman and to complete the rescue force a van of spare parts was driven by crewman Norman Ward. It was to take the Southport rescue effort 9 hours, often in driving rain and freezing sleet to reach their destination. Not to mention the fuel consumption of the two thirsty D.U.K.W. engines. They consumed a staggering one gallon to every five miles to travel to Lincolnshire, a total of around 60 gallons each just to get to the disaster site! Driving an open GMC D.U.K.W., with little or no weather protection in summer weather is not really for the faint hearted. To drive one to Lincolnshire from Southport on 1950s British roads in a car was bad enough, but in a 1940s WW II D.U.K.W.....

The actual task of getting aboard the nearly 8 foot height of the D.U.K.W.s hull, via the narrow footholds, can be quite challenging especially in wet conditions. Rankin solved this problem when operating his summer duck service. When his crewmen found themselves struggling to lift older members of the public up into his vehicles, Rankin simply had built a mobile ladder unit which could be wheeled to each vehicle to load and unload. Later the Lifeguards had a simpler version which doubled as a diving platform.

Under the hood of the WW II amphibian is a D.U.K.W.s GMC model 270 six cylinder engine. To the observer, the size of the engine, in comparison to the overall mass of the rest of the D.U.K.W's huge body, would seem to make the war veteran somewhat underpowered.

**D.U.K.W. Engine**

Appearances, however, can be deceptive. Once on the road a D.U.K.W., (either on the level road or climbing up at a reasonable angle), can reach a respectable 50mph. The driver has a lever to the 5 speed manual gearbox on the floor by his right leg, remembering that all the US vehicles are left hand drive. The drive power is through the front wheels but can then be converted to 4x4 and then 6x6 to adjustments to the transfer case. Drivers sometimes comment on the noise which comes vibrating from the gearbox case, once the elaborate gears and shafts swing into action.

Rankin's crews driving to Lincolnshire on England's 1953 East coast roads would have had to get used to the restricted forward view from the cab. Though the driver's position is reasonably elevated in relation to the road, the driver's position is inboard of the hull and equally distant from the curved front of the vehicle. One useful aid to driving is the position of the headlights. They are positioned directly over the wheels, so the driver knows exactly where they are.

When the D.U.K.W. is in its natural environment (in water), the amphibians' general noise level is substantially reduced and driver vision much improved.

Before entering the water the D.U.K.W's driver must engage the propeller unit.

This is done by depressing the clutch pedal and engaging the floor lever to "DRIVE". One technique to help with sea going performance is to keep the road wheels turning even when travelling through water. This was not a technique always adopted by civilian drivers.

Once a D.U.K.W. is driven out of any water environment, it has to be paused, to disengage the propeller from the main drive. Due to the amphibians' famous low freeboard and open cargo bay the designers seemed to have anticipated that their new creation would probably ship challenging amounts of water during operations. Thanks to the effective power of the bilge pumps, the safety and reliability of the D.U.K.W. was kept in high regard by both military and civilian crews. This system, designed to try and make it difficult for the D.U.K.W. to be overwhelmed by any inundation of water into its hull, was a system of three pumps units. Two of these were powered and the other one was hand operated. The main pumps were designed to start automatically when the water level in the bilges reached 250mm (25 centimeters). Together, all the pump units could cope with a high level of flooding. To test this system under realistic conditions during the D.U.K.W.s preproduction trials, a 75mm shell was fired through the body of a vehicle to test the pumps to their full capacity! This dramatic test situation proved beyond doubt the bilge pumps were able to cope with a flow of 180 gallons per minute.

We return to the small town of Mabelthorpe, in Lincolnshire where the newly arrived Southport D.U.K.W.s and their crews were getting acquainted with the daunting task that now confronted the salvage crews sent to the disaster area. For miles and miles around the duck's base, villages and towns were partially submerged beneath a combination of muddy water, silt and sand. The sand in particular choked streets, buildings, rivers and indeed anything it could penetrate however well protected. Streets were filled with broken down cars, lorries and any other vehicles that had been out on that terrible night.

The Southport rescue team was deployed to many different emergency situations. This included the rescue of many marooned and starving farm animals. In one such incident a huge bull had to be winched on an A frame aboard one of the vehicles, despite the fact it had gone half mad in the harsh conditions. Joe and his crew had to snatch a few hours sleep here and there, often in very make shift accommodation including a church hall and a police cell. It soon became very clear that two D.U.K.W.s were just not going to be enough for the size of the job on hand, so Joe sent for 4 more vehicles and another van full of spares. It took time to get the reinforcements into place. Back in the flood zone, the strain was telling on both men and machines. Nobody realised that the rescue effort would find the rescuers working night and day for six weeks with little time to recharge their own batteries.

During this period of intense effort there was an unexpected visitor, whose very active presence was to act as a considerable boost to all those engaged in the flood relief effort. That celebrity was none other than the newly appointed Admiral of the Fleet H.R.H. the Duke of Edinburgh. The Duke, despite his newly married status and the Coronation year, paid a number of visits to the East Coast in support of the victims and relief force. During one of his visits he was reunited with Joseph Rankin fellow officers in the Royal Navy. (Joe was actually in the R.N.R,) The Duke was taken in Dragonfly on a tour of the worst areas. He was visibly distressed at the amount of damage and the suffering by the local people. Clad in borrowed sea boots, the Duke covered some of these devastated towns and villages both walking and in the D.U.K.W. Indeed, such was his pace, it was reported, that many of the press core had considerable difficulty keeping up with him!

After nearly six weeks, Joe and four of his vehicles returned to Southport leaving two vehicles behind to help in the final part of the clearing up operation. A new summer season was just around the corner and Joe had to fulfil his contract with Southport Corporation to supply vehicles for that contract. He had committed nearly a third of his D.U.K.W. fleet to the emergency relief effort and now they were all in pretty bad shape. Rankin expressed his view, in an interview with the Southport Visiter on his return, that what he and his men had witnessed during the East Coast flood operation, would remain in their memories for many years to come.

## A FEW OF THE MANY OTHER EVENTS RECORDED IN THE SOUTHPORT VISITER AND GUARDIAN OF 1953./54

It was recorded on the sixth of May in 1953 in the Southport Visiter that a visitor's dog, chasing sea gulls on the beach, did not notice those crafty creatures of the air, gradually getting their revenge by leading the animal on to a sandbank. Not unusual in itself had it not been for a rapid incoming tide. The combined efforts of the Police, RSPCA, and a D.U.K.W. were required to rescue the now frightened animal marooned on a shrinking hill of sand. No gulls to be seen!

On the last day of June the Southport Guardian reported the tragic news of a Schoolboy feared lost in the sea. Eight-year-old Derick Cooper mysteriously disappeared near the Pinfold Channel while on a school trip. D.U.K.W.s were involved in the search dragging the channel with grappling hooks. He was presumed dead and confirmed when the search failed to find him. Only after a week had passed was his body found on the beach.

23rd JULY: A D.U.K.W. driver dived from his vehicle while at sea to rescue a 16-year-old swimmer in trouble off the Ainsdale coast. The driver tied a rope to himself and to the vehicle's steering wheel to avoid it drifting away. A Successful rescue was the result of his actions.

31st_AUGUST 54 (VISITER) Visitor walking across the Horsebank to the sea, caught in soft sand up to the knees. Spotted by Southport Corporation D.U.K.W. driver and pulled aboard minus shoes.

6th SEPTEMBER 54 (VISITER/GUARDIAN) Shrimping cart sinking in quick sand, D.U.K.W. unable to save the cart but horse and owner led to safety behind the amphibious vehicle using its marine anchor and winch.

### col plate D. U. K. W. Salvaging BUOY

The harsh winter gales caused buoys belonging to the Mersey Docks and Harbour board to break free from their moorings. Joe Rankin's D.U.K.W.s were busy recovering or securing them to avoid any dangers from the drifting structures. Q16 (weighing 30tons and 52 feet in height) secured and landed after 4 D.U.K.W.s were deployed carrying a total of 12 salvage workmen equipped with Hawsers, Sea Anchors and Lifebelts. A Mersey docks salvage tug stood by to take the wandering buoy in tow, but the sea was too rough and shallow for it to be used. (these illustrations should go with article text in 1954)

The D.U.K.W. ELIZABETH was driven by Joe Rankin, the VIGILANT crewed by Cliff Bond, in the Albatross was Tom Sanderson, in the D.U.K.W. SWORDFISH Tony Righton. The Q16 struck the Vigilant breaking the tow rope. Another hawser was secured to the ELIZABETH who eventually towed the Q16 ashore, taking 2 hours to cover 2 miles. The Swordfish became stuck on a sandbank. T. Righton had to walk over a mile in water often waist high to get back to shore. SWORDFISH was recovered the next day.

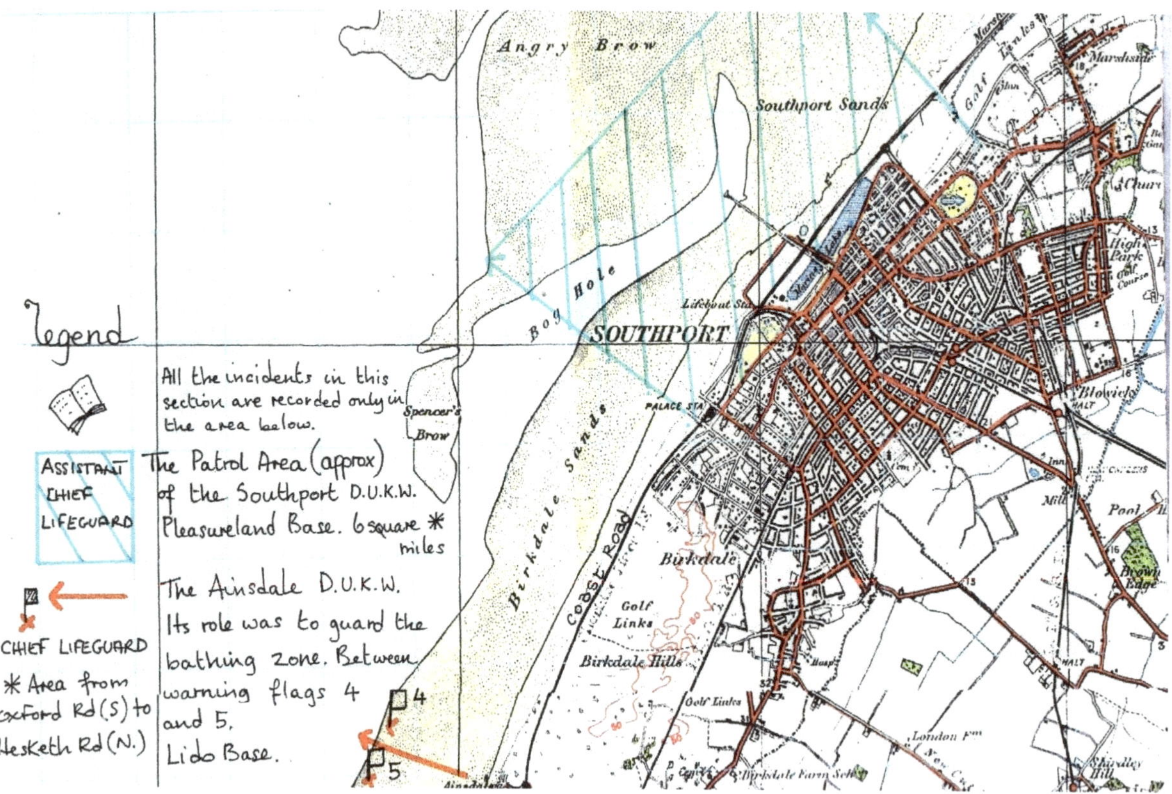



**D. U. K. W. Patrol Areas from 1953 onwards**

As the year 1953 came to a close Southport Publicity and Attractions Committee opened negotiations with Joseph Rankin to extend the D.U.K.W. patrols in the 1954 season to one hour before low water and five hours after low water from Easter to the end of September. The D.U.K.W.s were to replace the four foot patrolmen who were to be retrained as part of the new vehicle based rescue service.

The RSPCA Special Service Medal was also awarded to Joe, Hilton Steinman and N. Ward for their rescue work with animals during the winter floods on the East coast. We are not sure if the dog marooned on the sandbank was included in the roll call.

The year was, however, not over for the rescue service quite yet. Three articles from the Visiter and the Guardian covered the D.U.K.W.'s successful involvement in the rescue of two children marooned on the Horsebank. They were attempting to walk to Blackpool! Regretfully both these two youngsters, as many before and after this incident, failed to know that two major, watery barriers were standing in their way these being the River Douglas and the greater Ribble Estuary. On the previous Tuesday the same D.U.K.W. pulled a man from the sea off Ainsdale and so ended 1953.

## 1954

### Strong force 6 gales blowing S. Westerly early in the <u>New Year</u>

1st Jan 54. (Guardian).Marker buoys in the Mersey take the full force of the festive winter storms battering the North-West coastline.

A Second recovery of the MD&HB eight ton, 20ft high buoy Jordan's Split was attempted by two of Rankin's D.U.KWs. This attempt at recovery was postponed after one of the vehicles was rammed by the rogue buoy and had to be towed back to Liverpool docks by the second vehicle.

7th July 54. (Visiter and Guardian). Two boys trapped on the Horsebank. Miles Knox (12) and his brother Colin (7) from County Durham, rescued by a corporation patrol D.U.K.W. off the Horsebank. While walking across the shore to the sea, they were both caught in soft sand and sank to their knees. Spotted by D.U.K.W. driver Clifford Bond. Pulled to safety minus most of their clothes!

November/December. (Guardian/Visiter). (images in last section) Buoys adrift again **in the Mersey** channel causing a danger to the busy shipping lane.. The harsh winter gales caused buoys belong to the Mersey Docks & Harbour Board to break free from their moorings. Joe Rankin's D.U.K.W.s were soon busy recovering or securing them to avoid any dangers from the drifting structures. Q16 (weighing 30 tons and 52 feet high) secured and landed after 4 D.U.K.W.s were deployed carrying a total of 12 salvage workmen equipped with Hawsers, Sea Anchors and Lifebelts. A Mersey Docks salvage tug stood by to take the wandering buoy in tow, but the sea was too rough and shallow for it to be used. The D.U.K.W. 'Elizabeth' was driven by Joe Rankin, the 'Vigilant' crewed by Cliff Bond, in 'Albatross' was Tom Sanderson, in the D.U.K.W. 'Swordfish' Tony Righton. This vehicle became stuck on a soft sandbank, and Tony had to walk over a mile in water often waist high to get back to shore. The 'Swordfish' was recovered the next day.

Three other buoys including the P1 (Preston Channel) landed opposite Formby and River Alt later towed back to the Mersey.

## 1955

During the Summer season of 1955 the D.U.K.W. rescue service was kept busy with many routine recoveries and rescues. The north Southport patrol ducks' crew now had a further extension of two hours to its working day during the season April to September.

This required them to be in position by 8am and the day finished at 6.00pm. Lunch break was taken on the D.U.K.W. when and if time became available. By this period most crews consisted of three to four members, one of these being the vehicles driver.

Interestingly, though there was an increasing schedule for the training of the Lifeguards on board, this did not apply to the drivers. A D.U.K.W. driver seemed then, and for some period afterwards, to carry a kind of detached mystic! This was perhaps because they drove the amphibian and the guards carried out the rescues. It was thus that there were times when a driver who could not swim was at the helm (sorry steering wheel). It was a question nobody seemed to ask them, Can you swim?

**Lifeguards in Training**

There are no records of the loss of any drivers I am glad to say!

The 4th July. (Daily Dispatch/Liverpool Echo/Daily Telegraph).

This incident severely tested the Southport rescue service that year and the effective use of their unusual rescue vehicle. This event was the rescue of the 12 ton yacht Penboch. This large pleasure vessel suddenly struck a sandbank named Dead Man's Graveyard four miles off Southport. Pounded by heavy seas the yacht keeled over onto her side and began filling with water. Its wooden main mast then broke injuring one of the crew. The boat became wrapped in its own rigging and sails. The crew of three men and two boys were first rescued by the Lytham St Annes' lifeboat. The vessel was salvaged by J. Rankin driving one of the D.U.K.W.s supplied to the rescue service. Several visits had to be made to the wreck in the worst weather conditions seen for years, as she shed both cargo and wreckage. The wreck of the Penboch had to be then towed to safer waters and secured with anchors until the tide retreated and she could be properly salvaged. She was on a pleasure cruise from Northwich to Beaumaris. The whole incident was not resolved until the early hours of the following day.)

19th July (Visiter/Guardian) Boy rescued from drowning by a Mystery Girl. D.U.K.W. brings five year old Keith Baylor ashore from off the pier after an unknown girl dragged him unconscious from the water.

27th July. D.U.K.W.s assist in the search for a missing nine year old girl Hazel Wolstenholme without success.

You Cannot Keep a good D.U.K.W. down. The Call of <u>the Big Screen.</u>

During 1954 and early 1955 saw a brief, but rather amusing interlude for Joe Rankin and his men.

He was approached by a representative of the Rank film organisation concerning a film they were working on. "Dangerous Cargo" was a melodramatic, black and white cops and robbers 1950s crime film, starring some of the Rank Organisation's regulars including Nigel Patrick, Elizabeth Sellars, Terence Morgan, Jack Warner and Joyce Grenfell. The plot was based around the efforts of a rather suave, clean cut Narcotics agent (Nigel Patrick) on the trail of a gang of drug smugglers trying to use the English open coastline to land their goods, with the efforts of the police aided by eccentric birdwatcher (Joyce Grenfell).Rank approached Joe with the idea of using a D.U.K.W. as the main vehicle that is used to bring the drugs ashore. Joe was delighted to oblige.

Especially as the money was not bad and it was a couple of weeks work. Even better, Joe negotiated that some of his staff should have minor parts in the film! Skilled hands were needed at the D.U.K.W.'s controls.

● JOE Rankin (far left) keeps a watchful eye on his men unloading recovered cargo as part of a scene from the J Arthur Rank film 'Forbidden Cargo' which was shot on Ainsdale beach around 1950. My thanks to Arthur MacCannon for the loan of these great scenes.

Film stills: Dangerous Cargo

Thus five of Joe's employees, including James Biddolph, Arthur McGannon, Dougie Price and Cliff Bond (and Joe) found themselves in British Navy ratings uniforms being pursued by the forces of law and order. Their part, quite small in the overall scheme of things, was filmed on Ainsdale beach, and Joe acted as driver for most of his part. The film, 83 minutes long and entitled "Dangerous Cargo" (a Story Box Production) hit the screens in 1954 without, I regret to say, any of Rankin's budding stars appearing on the credits! As far as I know it failed to garner any Oscar nominations although, I believe that you can still get copies of the film via the internet.

By 1958 the post war boom in the British summer holiday trade was beginning to show signs of bottoming out. This decline was to soon reach the holiday towns of the North of England. The reasons behind this change of fortunes can be linked to a number of parallel changes in the recreational habits of the population. One of the most far reaching can be witnessed right up to today. The cheap package tour, with its near guarantee of good weather, drew holiday makers away from windswept British resorts, and towards foreign destinations, geared up to the Beer, Fish and Chips desires of their new clients.

Joe Rankin saw these early signs and acted accordingly. He already had plans of branching out into the fiberglass industry. He had experimented with this material in the repairing of his D.U.K.W.s. Consequently, in 1958 he sold his D.U.K.W. leisure business to an up and coming local engineering company Thompson & Doxey Export Ltd. He then opened his new fiberglass supply company, Glasplies Ltd, where he continued in business until into his early 80s, only retiring after a number of small strokes!

Thompson & Doxey Export Ltd was founded by two Southport brothers Roy and Tony Thompson. They first opened their doors for business in the late 1950s, sharing their father Reg's workshop. They soon moved the company to a much larger facility on the Southport/Ormskirk A570 highway, about a mile from the Southport border.

The Thompson family were themselves by no means new to the vehicle repair and maintenance world. As mentioned, their father Reg had opened his own business of Thompson & Doxey Engineering, with his partner and brother-in-law Gerald Doxey, in 1931.

After opening their workshops in Sefton Street, a showroom in Eastbank Street at the bottom of the hill, was added to the firm. Reg Thompson went on to make a bit of a name for himself as a competition rider and driver on the beaches of Ainsdale and Southport. An activity which became associated in the 1920s and 30s with such colourful legends as Sir Henry Segrave, Capt Malcolm Campbell and the band leader Billy Cotton.

**1953/54 Derby Road goods yard**
**Thompson and Doxey company shipping D.U.K.W.s to Las Palmas 1950s"**
**By Dick Taylor (Chief Goods Clerk)**

The Thompson brothers formed their company to concentrate solely on the import/export and refurbishing of ex-military vehicles for a newly expanding civilian market. The idea of making money from the military surplus business had been a sideline for father Reg. He had started bringing surplus vehicles into Southport as early as 1949. In that year he sent mechanics from his engineering business to pick up vehicles from Southampton docks. They were brought back on low loader lorries supplied by local toffee magnate John Holland of Holland Toffee fame! (you remember the Penny Arrow?) vehicles waiting for export to Las Palmas in 1954.

If you stood outside the premises of the Thompson brothers' new company, one would quickly spot vehicles that could be the bread and butter of any decent war film! The American Willys and Ford jeeps, 4x4 Dodge trucks, GMC 6x6 trucks, Studebaker Rio heavy recovery vehicles and of course D.U.K.W.s rumbled out of their plant after being refurbished and prepared for civilian life. There was to be many a local lad who would serve his engineering apprenticeships working on those future icons in the T&D workshops.

1950s Refurbished M38 jeeps outside Thompson and Doxey Export LTD

To maintain a healthy supply of vehicles for their newly formed company, the Thompson brothers travelled to American bases and Government Surplus sales to acquire vehicles and spare parts. Even into the 50s and early 60s the flow of such hardware, much of it mothballed since the war years in depots in Britain and across Europe, showed little sign of diminishing! Ray and Tony had these purchases driven back, either transported on low loaders or just occasionally by rail. Once these vehicles were brought up to civilian specifications they were either sold directly or auctioned. It was pretty amazing just what you could buy from T&D in those days and the prices you would pay.

Tony Thompson tries the controls of a heavy lifter.
Brother Roy looks on.  1960
By M. Biddolph

I remember talking to a military motorbike enthusiast who went to one of these auctions in the late 1950s. He read in a trade magazine that their auction included a number of American military Harley Davidson motorbikes. He duly went. He put in his bid for £75. After the auction an employee asked the enthusiast where he wanted the (unopened) crates delivering. The surprised winner replied that he had only put in one bid. The reply was "That's right, Your lot was three Harleys, all unpacked in crates".

1950s. Outside workshop of Thompson & Doxey Exports Ltd. Southport Road.

James Biddolph standing alongside a ex-US Army M108 Studebaker R10

(James Biddolph Collection)

(DUKW Disc 1.)

D.U.K.W. outside Linaker St. School early 1950s. Taken by J. Biddolph from Dodge weapons carrier.

(James Biddolph Collection)

(DUKW Disc 1)

Willys Jeeps lined up outside Linaker St. School, Linaker St. early 1950s.

(James Biddolph Collection)

(DUKW. Disc 1)

**Thompson and Doxey Engineering**

Rankin's last remaining D.U.K.W.s went to Doxeys in 1958. The company then negotiated a contract with the old Southport Corporation to continue to supply them with D.U.K.W.s and parts for the beach rescue service. This included the servicing of these units and their complete refurbishment in the off season. Southport and then later Sefton Metropolitan District Council, usually retained a minimum of three D.U.K.W.s on their inventory, two on station at Southport and Ainsdale and one in reserve.

One of the founder members of the T&D team was James Biddolph. He was already an experienced career mechanic and apprentice of father Thompsons Engineering workshops in Sefton Street. However, when Regs' two sons opened their business they persuaded Jim to join them in 1958 with the rank of workshop foreman. Though a quiet and low key person, it would appear in conversation with his widow Margaret, that he had an eventful career at Thompsons. Once in true Rankin tradition, the Thompson brothers sent him to Venice with spare parts to help in a period of the disastrous flooding which periodically plagues that great city.

One of Rankin's early customers were the monks of Calder Island near Tenby. They needed such a vehicle to get to their Monastery! Apparently, without one they didn't stand a prayer! The brothers were pretty handy with a spanner and really looked after their vehicles. Ray and Tony honoured the contract and when their old Rankin vehicle came to the end of its working life they duly dispatched foreman Jim in a refurbished D.U.K.W. to keep the monks afloat. God appears to work in very mysterious ways.

Nothing ever left the workshops of T&D without first being tested. With their D.U.K.W.s this required a water test in the sea off the Southport or Ainsdale shore. These did not always go as planned. Late in 1958 Jim Biddolph, Tony, Reg and Ray Thompson set out in two vehicles on a sea conditions test. A sudden thick mist engulfed them and much fuel was used as they became totally disorientated. Tony Thompson decided to transfer fuel from one vehicle to the other. The cap on the D.U.K.W.'s fuel tank, however, got jammed, and as Tony Thompson struggled to loosen it, the cap suddenly snapped open spraying him with petrol, especially his face and hair. The rest of the crew sprang into action, turned Tony upside down and gripping him by the ankles, dipped him into the sea! It did the job! Back on shore, Mrs Thompson had contacted the police as her husband and sons were well overdue. The lights on both Southport and New Brighton piers were switched on to act as beacons, and after many hours the exhausted men were picked up by the Liverpool dredger the Astland. What should have been a routine test run turned into a fog bound nightmare. But, all in a days work.

During the early 1960s two of the Thompson's senior mechanics Chris Trees and Rod Taylor told me of another incident involving Ray and Tony, who had been called out to help with the salvage of a new wreck in the Mersey Channel. There was some confusion on the state of the tides in the Mersey at that time of the year, but the Thompsons apparently despite some advice decided to position one D.U.K.W. directly over the wreck! A rapid fall in the sea level, as the ebb tide flowed away, caught the Thompsons by surprise. The vehicle with Roy aboard struck the wreck, a piece went through the floor and the vehicle sank like a stone. Roy just got out with seconds to spare. The two brothers returned the next day. They hoped to recover their lost vehicle, but it was not to be, just as they had winched the D.U.K.W. almost to the surface, it again caught on the wreck, rolled over and sank into deep water.

THE LATE JAMES BIDDULPH DOXEY'S CHIEF MECHANIC DURING THE 1950s. STANDING BY A DODGE WEAPONS CARRIER WW2 VINTAGE. HE WAS TO DIE IN THE SERVICE OF DOXEY'S. (MARGARET BIDDULPH. D.UKW. TAPE 1)

### James Biddolph 1950

Jim Biddolph departed on the 12th March 1967 to a US airbase in Cambridgeshire to collect a D.U.K.W. for Thompsons. Doing the job he loved most he died at the wheel from a massive heart attack during the return journey. Roy Thompson was killed in an automobile accident and this led to the closure of the company in 1975.

By that year much of the maintenance of Sefton's fleet of D.U.K.W.s had passed into the control of the local government.

James Biddolph - Wreck of Doxey D.U.K.W.

## Lifeguards and Sea Rangers

Before the first steel bodied D.U.K.W.s plunged into our grey, shallow sea on their many missions of life and death, there was an uncharted age. Between the closing of the lifeboat station in 1925 to 1949, I can find no records or evidence of an official inshore rescue service from Formby to the Ribble Estuary other than the lifeboats of the RNLI. During this period there were coastal conditions that began to alter, the environment of the North- West coastline. These changes made this part of England's coast less hazardous to both man and machine. Ships in the Mersey and the Ribble Estuaries no longer depended on the power of sail. This made them less vulnerable to the unpredictable nature of wind and tide, forces which were the downfall of many a sailing ship.

Steel ships replaced those of wood and the improvement in navigation technology further reduced human error. Reduction in water quality and some overfishing were among numerous factors leading to fewer and fewer local fishing boats as fish and shellfish stocks declined.

Up to the 1920s and 30s the idea of the British seaside holiday was not a common reality for the lower income British citizen. The inventions that really got a revolutionary level of mobility into the lives of countless working class families was firstly the railways, then between World War One and Two the affordable family motor car. Railways had played a major role in this social movement, but once one got your sprawling family to the station, you then had to trudge some distance to the shore. The small family car could cut the cost by travelling to a resort for the day, allowing Dad to be back at work on Monday!

Just when Southport was enjoying this cultural and financial boom, its reputation as a classy holiday town growing throughout the 1930s, a black cloud descended. Adolf Hitler was not the man to appreciate the holiday industry. Dark days fell across Britain, Europe and much of the globe. During the Second World War the beaches of Ainsdale, Birkdale and Southport were turned over to the three services. They were not returned to civilian ownership until late 1945 or early 1946, and as previously mentioned it took until 1950 to get the Ainsdale beach back into a suitable state for sea bathing.

With the new D.U.K.W. rescue service it soon became clear that a new kind of sea rescue unit to crew these vehicles, was going to be needed. There was already a need for lifeguards at the newly reopened Outdoor Swimming Pool. The Pool, for years an Icon of Southport, became the centre for training lifeguards. The rank of beach Superintendent was created and offices to organise and run all shore activities were established in the main Pleasure Land car park. The first lifeguards, recruited in the late 1940s, patrolled the beach on foot, their patrol zone covering the beach from

Pleasure Land car park to an outstanding beachside luxury facility called The Palace Hotel, to the South of the Borough in Birkdale. The Lifeguards would then revert to a northern route along the beach to the end of Southport's huge man -made lake, the Marine Lake to the North. They alternated duties on the beach with those lifeguards at the Outdoor Pool, but the Leisure Services soon discovered that sole reliance on foot patrols did not meet the needs of a growing beach population which in turn led to the growing number of beach related incidents. The introduction of the amphibious D.U.K.W. as the backup for the lifeguards began an evolution which was to lead to the use of that vehicle for much longer than I think even the most far sighted official of the Leisure Services department could ever have imagined.

1952 .Arthur McGannon standing by Southport Corporation dukw no 2.
All grey livery and single title on side. (photo C&P Mc Gannon)

With this increased tourist activity a new post of Chief Lifeguard was created in the early 1950s.the first of these was a certain Chris Rae.

Regretfully the author, despite some effort, was unable to unearth any personal details of Southport's first Chief Lifeguard. A pity as it would seem that Chris Rae laid the first foundations of integrating the lifeguards with the new D.U.K.W.s and thus also laying the foundations for the Sea Rangers. As I have already mentioned, the D.U.K.W.s first lifeguard crews and their drivers, were Rankin's own employees. They in turn trained employees of the Southport Leisure Services. However, some of

Rankin's men stayed on as permanent employees of Southport Corporation after the Tourism Department took over, following Rankin's withdrawal. It was in the second period between 1953 and 1973 that the Lifeguard Service really came of age. Thanks to the efforts of Chris Rae and then his successor Verdi Godwin they began the process of converting a small band of individuals into an elite team.

**Right: Chief Verdi Godwin awarded BEM**

Verdi Godwin joined the Southport Lifeguards under the leadership of Chris Rae in 1957. If there were any particular qualities that our guardians of the shoreline possessed they were considerable toughness and an alert awareness to changing conditions and situations. New recruit Verdi was one of the first of the new breed of Lifeguards and the talents that secured his place in their ranks, he had developed since he was a boy. Verdi was born in Blackburn the son of a weaver. His early years were a struggle with unemployment and the poverty that dogged a declining textile industry. As his parents could not afford the price of the local swimming baths Verdi learnt to swim in the Leeds/Liverpool canal! The canal was not known for the quality of its water. Neither were there too many places where you could put your feet down if you got into difficulties. At the age of 17 he was recruited by Blackburn Rovers FC playing centre forward. He played for both Manchester and Stoke City football clubs. The Second World War inflicted its influence on Verdi. He found his name on the

National Ballot list, when he became a Bevan boy and was sent to work as a miner in the war effort. After working an eight-hour shift down the pit he would cycle twenty miles to go training at Blackburn and then back again. By 1950, after a period at Tranmere Rovers FC, he became a scout for the legendary Bill Shankly. An advert in the Southport Visiter for Lifeguards for the 1957 season came to Verdi's attention. He applied and Chris Rae quickly recognised Verdi's qualifications for the post and recruited him straight away.

Verdi had hardly been two years in the employment of Southport Leisure and Tourism when Chris Rae retired, and Verdi found himself in the position of Chief Lifeguard. He turned his organising abilities to putting the service on a more professional footing and closely co-ordinating the D.U.K.W.s and Lifeguards. This service became organised around two teams. One based at the Lido in Ainsdale and the second at the Pleasure Land car park on Southport's Marne Drive. Each team had one D.U.K.W. at its disposal while a third was in reserve. D.U.K.W. drivers, though part of the team, always had a certain exclusive quality. But the roles of Lifeguards and drivers was designed to become interchangeable. Chief Lifeguards were always part of the driving team and as the years went along there were to be more than a few cases when D.U.K.W. drivers took an active role in rescues.

A shift system for both Lifeguards and Drivers was introduced, although, due to the workings of the tides, a certain flexibility had to be built into this system. A Lifeguards shifts was generally 9.00am to 5.00pm and the second shift 2.00pm to 6.00pm during a season which lasted from the first day in April to the last day of September.

Lifeguards worked a six day week with one day's rest, and in the 1950s and early 60s were paid the handsome salary of £8-10s-0d a week, however if you were the proud owner of the Bronze Life Saving Medal you received £9 a week. The D.U.K.W. driver's shift system was based on a similar schedule. They worked from 9.30am to 3.30pm and the second shift was 3.30pm to 9.30pm. This later time reflected the various after-service checks required on a D.U.K.W. to get it ready for the next day's patrol. These were part of a driver's duties. The pay salary of a driver mirrored that of a lifeguard.

**The first D.U.K.W. Patrols off Southport & Ainsdale**
**Refurbished D.U.K.W. outside T&D, ready for action**
**as part of the Southport Corporation Fleet. (C. Trees)**

1. They were based at the Beach Superintendent's Offices. Their patrol area limit to the Palace Hotel.

2. Rankin's D.U.K.W.s were based at Southport & Ainsdale in 1951. They had a vehicle which patrolled the Horsebank to opposite Marshside. Another D.U.K.W. at the Ainsdale Lido.

3. Southport Corporation took over Rescue D.U.K.W.s. Official base at Ainsdale. Patrol area extended to the Formby barrier. Patrols on foot and jeep. Southport patrol area same as pioneered by Rankin. Three of Joe Rankin's employees who continued to work for the Leisure and Tourism Department as D.U.K.W. drivers were Kevin Stringfellow, Cliff Bond and Arthur McGannon. Over the coming years there would be many more who served in the red and yellow of the lifeguards, I regret that no official records exist as to all of their names. I will mention as many as I can or know of in the following pages. I can only apologise to the many worthy individuals who I have failed to include.

Among the early recruits, destined to play a long term role was Italian Tony Venurini. Before arriving on the windswept beaches of the North-West of England, Tony was to see a period as a Border guard for his native country. He became a waiter at the famous Palace Hotel, then, like so many others spotted an advert in the Southport Visiter. He applied and went for his lifeguard test under the watchful eye of new Chief Lifeguard, Verdi Godwin.

Once again the test was at the outdoor pool in March. Water temperature in the outdoor pool at that time of the year was, was, well…enough to freeze……!! Tony informed me that he had to swim at least three lengths of the Lake. I am not acquainted with the dimensions of the pool, but if my fading memory serves me correctly it was either cold, very cold or.... All three swimming strokes were tested.

Then there were extra lengths using just arms on their own and legs, without use of the arms. Tony passed and was patrolling the beach as a guard until 1959. He then transferred to the D.U.K.W. drivers' squad, and together with the vehicles to which he devoted a fair portion of his life until retired from service in 1998.

Deputy Lifeguard chief Bill Doherty on the deck of another early vehicle in the DUKW fleet. No official uniforms and no official title could mean this vehicle was a reserve vehicle. .(image found in a rubbish bin when the Rangers office was demolished !) 1960s

Chief Lifeguard Verdi Godwin, spent much of his career based at the Ainsdale base at the Lido building, and I am indebted to ex-lifeguards Tommy James, Paul Schunke and Tony Venturini as well as Verdi himself for these memories and observations. The first presence of a D.U.K.W. at Ainsdale, for the sole purpose of being part of the Lifeguard service, was due to the first unofficial deal between Rankin and Southport Tourism and Attractions in the 1950s.

The waters off the Lido were first officially opened to the public for bathing in 1952, and again, a Rankin supplied amphibian, crewed by his employees and lifeguards began the service. From 1953 onwards the Ainsdale D.U.K.W.s began their season at the beginning of April through to the last day of September. For several years, no one was quite sure just how long, both the Southport and Ainsdale vehicles were based at the Beach Superintendent's Offices on the old Pleasure land car park, with the latter D.U.K.W. being driven to its Lido base each morning, but it was a system which proved both costly in fuel and time, and the D.U.K.W.s mechanical condition, often without a main braking system due to water/sand incursion, meant road journeys were best kept to a minimum. The Ainsdale vehicle, thus ended up parked beside the First Aid and Lost Children's building during the week.

DUKW No 11 ON DUTY AT
THE PIER STATION. A TYPICAL
SOUTHPORT LATE SUMMER'S DAY
IN THE 80's    (K. STRINGFELL

A RANGER'S DUTY.
FRANK WALSH ORGANISES
THE LOADING OF BEACH
WARNING FLAGS ABOARD A
SEATON DUKW.
(K. STRINGFELLOW)

The system used to patrol the Ainsdale section of the beach, from the old Palace Hotel to the Formby barrier, used both D.U.K.W. and foot patrols (the Palace Hotel backed onto the Fisherman's Rest on Weld Road and extended virtually to Oxford Road). The Ainsdale vehicle acted as a mobile base for the lifeguards. The Rangers vehicle would mainly stand close to the flagged area (red/yellow) which indicated the official safe bathing zone. The vehicle would then follow the tide out to its furthest point of its ebb. This patrol zone terminated as far as a rising hill of sand aptly named The Horsebank. If the tide was on the flow, however, the lifeguards would move in to round up stragglers and guide swimmers to the safe swimming areas. The greatest danger which the beach patrols faced was members of the public either being caught on a sandbank or cut off by the tide in soft sand or mud. These were hidden dangers which were to plague our shoreline, despite the outstanding efforts of the lifeguards and Shore Rangers.

Tommy James took on the mantle of Assistant Lifeguard at Ainsdale in the late 1950s, he commented that the posting was not the most popular in those days. This was a time when the ownership of private cars had not yet grown to huge levels of the later 1950s, There was no coastal road and so the Lido was therefore somewhat out on a limb. Being a lifeguard or a D.U.K.W. crew member meant you faced a daily shortage of basic facilities. There were just no toilets or washing facilities out there on those wind blown beaches.! There weren't any, especially if you were out on patrol It became a bit of a tradition, if that's the word one can best use, to use the limited facility of the D.U.K.W.! A desperate lifeguard would raise one of the internal floor boards and exposed the vehicles sump, into which one relieved oneself! With the constant supply of fresh air, this habit took a while to come to the surface, but during one of Verdi's inspections the resulting odour could no longer be hidden. The Chief Lifeguard ordered the vehicles' sea plugs to be removed and that she be driven into the sea to flush out the problem. At which point things suddenly went seriously wrong.

There was a change in shift, and those going off forgot to tell the next crew about the missing plugs. Next, the Southport D.U.K.W., while on a mission, BROKE DOWN. The Ainsdale D.U.K.W. was sent for. It came roaring down the beach at top speed and plunged into the sea, with the crew still unaware that the drainage plugs were missing. To the surprise of both crews, those awaiting rescue and bemused members of the public, the red and yellow war veteran sank. All that was left were the crew attempting to round up floating pieces of personal cargo, towels, swimming gear, sandwiches, deck chairs, etc. There followed a brief period of embarrassment. This was not helped by the presence of a Southport Visiter journalist who witnessed the entire, unfortunate episode! Thompsons' recovery vehicle soon turned out and salvaged the D.U.K.W., and she was back on station within the week, no doubt with a much chastened crew!

### Lifeguards in Training on the wreck of the American steamship SS ZEALANDIA

To be a lifeguard needed a certain sense of humour, of which the incident of the tailor's dummy is perhaps a prime example. Two unnamed lifeguards decided to deposit the said item of display under the pier, up to its neck in mud. They sat back to see what might develop, but not for long. Spotted by a pier walker the Police, Fire Brigade and rescue services were alerted. On finding the source of the alert, they did not see the funny side of the event. The lifeguards were handed a week's suspension from duty. Mention must be made of a few of the other talents which Verdi brought to the Southport summer scene during his three decades as Chief Lifeguard.

His pier diving exploits fit well into a tradition of pier divers doing back to Edwardian days! Verdi only carried out this activity when, of course, he was off duty, and like all responsible pier divers he knew the tides and the movement of the Bog Hole channel off the pier. These had to be right before a dive could be attempted, as of course was the state of the crowd. (There had to be one before any responsible diver risked life and limb, although granted it was a calculated risk). How many times Verdi plunged from the pier end into the muddy waters below, he is unsure. But he is sure that his dives followed the reputation of two local Edwardian Professors named Osbourne and Powsey who also clocked up an unrecorded number of successful plunges at the turn of the 20th century. Professor Powsey was still hitting the waves at the ripe old age of 73! Two other lifeguards, Peter Harrison and Jerry Ewell, also proved themselves capable of mastering the skill of plunging from the end of the pier.

Bill Doherty, Assistant Chief Lifeguard/Chief Lifeguard (1965-1997).

## Doherty Awards with Notes

In 1965 Chief Lifeguard Verdi Godwin signed up Bill Doherty who was to become one of the main pillars of first the Southport and later the Sefton Lifeguard Service which, by the mid 1960s, had a solid foundation which would serve it for another three decades. Bill Doherty was a Liverpool man. As a young boy he began to develop the kind of talents that later in life would stand him in good stead on the sea tossed decks of the red and yellow D.U.K.W.s At the age of just 14, Bill became the City of Liverpool 100 metres swimming champion and the City of Liverpool Catholic Schools swimming champion, breaststroke and backstroke. He held these for a couple of years. He later became an amateur boxer, but this got a little squeezed by Bill signing up for the Merchant navy in 1955 for the Cunard Line.

After his discharge from the Merchant Navy in 1961, Bill joined Southport Council, then in 1965 the ranks of the Southport Lifeguards. In the following he was raised to the rank of Assistant Chief Lifeguard. He was given overall responsibility for the Southport D.U.K.W. operation while Verdi continued at Ainsdale. Bill Doherty brought to the post of Assistant Chief Lifeguard, then later Chief Beach Supervisor, his own unique style. He was a man sensitive to the legacy that the Lifeguards and Shore Patrol as guardians of the North West shoreline. He was sensitive to the link between those oilskin clad lifeboat men who once walked our sands and those who followed in their footsteps. Evidence of those passed events can still be witnessed even today in the rotting timbers and barnacle encrusted ironwork of wrecked ships that all the lifeguards became familiar with on their patrols.

The combined skills of Verdi Godwin and Bill Doherty made the Southport and then the Sefton Lifeguards the skilled and outstanding service that graced our shores for nearly 40 years. They utilized the unique qualities of the WW II amphibious D.U.K.W., into a highly effective rescue vehicle. Such was the reputation that the rescue service was to establish, besides that of the numbers of people rescued, no vehicle or crew member was ever lost during its entire lifetime. In their hometown of Southport, our Victorian ancestors celebrated the deeds of those heroic lifeboatmen. They built monuments, put their image on the original town badge, wrote songs and poems about their deeds. In our twenty-first century, there is no such recognition of the lives saved by the men clad in red and yellow.

Reading the reports of the lifeguards and talking to the many that are still living around this town, one begins to sense an underlying yet respectful rivalry between their two Chiefs. This rivalry does not seem to have had any detrimental influence on the service, indeed, although they probably did not recognise it at the time, may well have been one of the reasons behind its success story! It is thanks to one of Bill Doherty's particular skills that we can appreciate the day to day actions and incidents faced by the lifeguards.

Bill's attention to detail contained in his incident reports, spanning the late 70s to the end of the Lifeguards in 1998 are the basis of this knowledge. These reports were the day to day communications that the service had with their bosses in the Tourism and Leisure Services. Luckily, being the man he was, Bill kept copies of a fair portion of this material. Otherwise, I fear it would have all been lost forever. Bill Doherty was also aware of the need for public awareness regarding the work of the lifeguards. If there was anyone who raised the reputation of the lifeguard and their D.U.K.W.s, often to national exposure on TV and in the press, it was the Assistant Chief Lifeguard.

During the 1960s and during the rest of this second period the responsibilities and duties of the lifeguards were clearly laid down through tried and tested circumstances. These regulations of service were firstly created under the old Southport Council and then from the 1970s onwards under Sefton MBC's Leisure Tourism and Attractions Department.

Sea Wolf (side view) showing built up sides to increase free board. Exhaust moved to rear through raised exhaust pipe. 1940s 'A' frame.

## The Lifeguards In Action

At the beginning of their weekly shifts both lifeguards and drivers checked in each shift at the Foreshore office which was situated on the car park. One of the routines was to check the incident report book covering the previous shift. Any outstanding issues from incidents on the last shift were then moved up the priority list. Next, the coastguard was contacted for an update on the weather for that day. This information alone could have a very profound influence on what kind of incidents might present themselves to the lifeguards during the current shift. Charts were then consulted to best plan that day's patrols. All the lifeguards were noted for their attendance.

**D.U.K.W. PREPARATION:** drivers had a checklist of maintenance schedules for their vehicles. For the Ainsdale D.U.K.W., enough fuel for the day had to be transported to the Lido base often in private cars. Then there was the D.U.K.W.'s water and oil levels to check and top up. Onboard equipment check was to make sure equipment was both present and sound. This included weather canvas, binoculars, first-aid equipment, throw lines, Torpedo buoys, etc. At the beginning of both the Ainsdale and Southport D.U.K.W.'s patrols, if the sea was at low tide, the lifeguards would make their way down to the Low water mark. From there the lifeguards could warn walkers and swimmers of the tide turning and beginning to flow. They would point out particularly the presence of sandbanks and their dangers. The areas designated as safe for bathing were indicated by red and yellow flags. Outside this limited zone, in the red flagged parts of the beach, lay a number of dangerous spots which had to be checked on a rota. One of these was at the end of the pier, where deep mud would be dragged up by the force of the tide down a shifting channel known as the Bog Hole. Storm outlets and manhole covers littered the beach and roads leading up to them, until removed in 1990.

The key element of a successful lifeguards and Ranger service lay in the training of the team. The physical and mental preparation that prepared the lifeguards for the season ahead, was the highest priority for both Verdi and Bill. There was a regular regime of sea training, lifesaving techniques, running on the beach and across the dunes.

D.U.KW. No 22 IN ITS FINAL SEASON
ON SOUTHPORT BEACH. (K. STRINGFELLOW)

K. Stringfellow

The two Chief Lifeguards used the D.U.K.W. in as many of these rehearsals as possible, mindful of the cost. The vehicle's legendary one gallon per mile in the water and 5 miles on land limited its use for too many practices. When the lifeguards were out training on the beach in wintery conditions, there were many members of the local public who viewed their efforts with a shudder. It was not a job for the faint hearted!

### Training Extraordinary

Sea born rescues were not events likely to go according to any well made plan. They are as unpredictable as the sea itself. Successful rescues from the lifeguards' amphibious D.U.K.W.s depended much on the skill of the driver to control the rolling vehicle in high winds and breaking waves.

Ready to start another tour of duty along South-port's golden sands is " Clem " Crouch, No. 1 shore ranger.

One of the well tried and tested techniques for picking up victims either in the sea or aboard a vessel was to bring the D.U.K.W. to a point where she was pointing into any wave action. The D.U.K.W. has only a few feet of hull above the water line so the driver is always concerned about flooding, totally reliant on the two bilge pumps tackling incoming water. But the engine must keep going. On the return trip the driver would swing his vehicle around and let her run with the tide. It was not unusual to strike unseen objects in the shallow sea, sandbanks being the most notorious. If this was to occur, drivers would sometimes engage the front wheel drive to drive the vehicle through the bank and to safety.

The Foreshore Inspectors beach operations were controlled from their offices which was also the main D.U.K.W. base. A second smaller office situated in the Lido complex at Ainsdale helped cover the South of the Borough. The role of the Foreshore Inspector was very clearly described on the job description originally set out by the Southport Borough department of Tourism and Attractions in the 60s and 70s. a statement of intent which proved to be still relevant when the Southport Borough was amalgamated into Sefton MBC on 1st__April 1974. The Foreshore

Inspector was responsible for the day to day management of the outside activities of the foreshore section with three other inspectors. Areas of control involved Lifeguards, Shore Patrolmen, Pier Staff, Car park attendants and general Attendants.

**Beach Inspector**
**Rankin's Recovery D.U.K.W. PN66**

The Foreshore inspector's official duty period was from April to September and this included duties on Saturdays, Sundays, Bank Holidays and some evenings! Thus his working week during that period was one of 44 hours of five and a half days. The period of October to March consisted of a 34-hour week. The essential qualifications for the job of Inspector, according to the official requirement, was a knowledge of the Southport Seafront as related to tourism activities, and the ability to control staffing and operational procedures. It went on to suggest that the role of inspector needed the gift of flexibility and initiative in dealing with unforeseen circumstances. It would appear that the last skill was the one most frequently called upon!

The Foreshore inspectors, from the early 50s until the 90s, wore a uniform which did not radically change in that period. The black jacket and trousers with peaked hat was the basic uniform. The jacket altered from a single breasted four buttons to a double breasted version. To show rank yellow stripes were worn on the arms; two for Chief Inspector and one for assistant. In the earlier uniform, that of the Southport Corporation, the jacket had four silver buttons and one on each breast pocket. Silver badges of the coat of arms were worn on the collar and the town crest on the hat badge. Sefton MBC modernised the look of the uniform, did away with the silver buttons but retained the authority emblem on the hat.

A rare photo of DUKWs 16 and 17 waiting to start their daily patrol.
Aboard Jim Walsh and Roger Cocker. (K.S.)

The last Southport DUKW no11 brand new in1973. The wet-suits were
being tried out to combat weather conditions. (KS)

One of the few written accounts of the life of a Foreshore Inspector comes from an article written in the 1970s by the then Chief Foreshore Inspector, Clement Taylor Crouch. Clement had moved from his home in Manchester to Southport in an attempt to improve a bout of bad health. After a brief period as a caretaker at Birkdale Congregational church he joined the ranks of the Beach patrol under the old Southport Corporation. In his article for a local magazine, found hidden in the papers of the late Bill Doherty, he gave an account of the Inspectors' activities. He recounts that he, together with two other inspectors, were responsible for the foreshore between Hesketh Road and Freshfield, an area of approximately six and a half miles each day, patrolled by Land-rover and on foot. His first shift lasted approximately nine hours, during the height of the season during April to October. The first shift began at 9am. First the Inspectors would drive along the tide line from the Pier to the Ainsdale Lido.

The main task was to look out for bodies either human or animal! Apparently, in the period just after the Second World War, amongst the vehicles used to patrol the beach was a motor bike and side car. This unusual combination proved to be the most practical when it came to the very disturbing task of removing bodies off the beach. The lifeguards were more than happy when this task later became the responsibility of the Police. Officer Clements other duties included keeping an eye out for stolen vehicles abandoned on the beach overnight. Another major task was dealing with the many children who got lost, injured or just generally separated from their parents on the beaches during the summer season. The Inspectors had to have a working knowledge of First Aid to treat problems like cut feet. That was of course the age when you were allowed to treat injured children. Later, when we entered the age of greater enlightenment, this activity was banned in case their parents sued the Local Authority for negligence.

The Inspectors also had to be on notice 24 hours a day during the season. Often at the end of a shift Clement would be called out to help with a rescue. Interestingly, despite this workload, Clement Taylor Crouch concluded his article by saying the job improved his health considerably. He enjoyed his career on the beach. He was replaced on his retirement by Fred Branchett who served his time as a D.U.K.W. driver, on the beach patrol and then as a Shore Inspector for Sefton MBC at Southport. In the 1990s the coastal service was re-organised and the ranks of Foreshore Inspectors abolished. The buildings themselves were demolished to make way for the bigger entertainment rides.

"Always on call, a brief break for a DUKW crew "
Left to Right: Frank Walsh,  Harry Drennar (driver),
Unnamed Crew member, and John Bond
Photo taken at Shore Ranger HQ 1989

# CHAPTER SIX

# THE THIRD AND FINAL PERIOD (1973 to 1998).

As mentioned Assistant Chief Lifeguard Bill Doherty spent most of his career in charge of the amphibious units at the Southport end of the Rangers' patrol zone. The Southport zone vehicle covered the coastal strip from the Ainsdale boundary to the afore mentioned old Rainsford Causeway. This also included what was known as the "Bank Patrol". During the season April to September this patrol was carried out at least once per day, depending on the tides. The Southport D.U.K.W. with a crew of designated Lifeguards would set out on a four mile round trip along the great sandbank named the Horsebank, northwards towards Blackpool. The purpose of the patrol was very much that of a preventative action. The D.U.K.W. would comb the sandbanks and often hidden gullies for those who had wandered from the main beach. Most of those who were found out on those deserted, dangerous areas were simply directed back to safe territory. This, however, was not always the case, and as we shall see, the "Bank Patrol" together with other units of the Shore patrol would only too frequently be called upon to help in incidents which did not always end happily.

During this third and final period from 1973 to 1998 the Sea Ranger service would encounter growing changes in their world from both an organisational and cultural perspective. Changes that would eventually herald the final days of the nearly five-decade service of the WW II D.U.K.W.s Perhaps the most influential of these changes to effect the Ranger service was to be the nature of the coastline itself. These physical alterations to the environment of the coastline were a combination of both natural and some man-made. Similar forces of nature and human intervention Lawson Booth witnessed with the end to the Southport Lifeboat Service in 1925 and of equal significance the changing habits of society itself.

As we get towards the end of this period, the fortunes of the man made GMC vehicle, would become another casualty of this inevitable tide of change.

## The second period 1953 to 1973
## Local Government Re-organisation.

A very significant event in the history of the North West coast was the end of the old Southport Borough Council together with many other traditional small councils in the local Government re-organizations of 1974. Southport Borough Council was amalgamated into the greater Merseyside creation of Sefton Metropolitan Council, and the department of Tourism was expanded. The new Sefton council, in the first decade of its existence, deployed four D.U.K.W.s in its fleet to serve both Ainsdale and Southport. These vehicles were employed on a rota system, with three on active duty while one was either in reserve or undergoing overhaul. A replacement vehicle was brought in about every other year, though this was a flexible arrangement depending entirely on deterioration of the vehicles in the fleet. At the end of a vehicle's active life, whether it was servicing with the old Southport Borough or later with Sefton, they were never sold off. Instead, each vehicle was cannibalised for their valuable spare parts. The hulls were then cut up for scrap.By the end of 1974, Sefton MBC's fleet of amphibious D.U.K.W.s included vehicle numbers 8, 9, 10 and 11.

Though the organisation of the Borough's may have changed, one thing that did not was the nature of the day to day problems faced by the crews of the D.U.K.W.s that patrolled the Southport and Ainsdale beaches. By the 70s and later the 80s, the habits of the visitors to seaside town like Southport had fundamentally changed. Britain, as a country, had put all its main transport eggs into one basket, and as a nation we had taken to the road. During the summer months, especially at the weekends, it was the day visitor who now took priority, the day visitor in the family car. The beaches in Southport became the focus of that day out and the revenue derived from virtual unlimited beach parking, did the coffers of the local authority no harm at all. During the months of June, July and August up to 5,000 cars a day, at weekends, would make their way along the crowded road network to the golden sands. There was no parking North of the Pier, but after that there were few parking restrictions. Consequently, it was much the task of the Rangers and Lifeguards to keep the forces of man and nature apart. This often was to prove a particularly thankless task, given the disregard some visitors had for, not only their own safety, but that of their own relatives and children. Not to mention that gleaming piece of engineering into which so much of their personal finance was sunk, the family automobile. The phrase sunk being a rather apt description on the fate that awaited not a small number on those unenlightened folks on those bright and sunny days. How could anything go wrong on the welcoming stretches of one of the North's premier seaside resorts? Especially the one, whom the Music Hall joke reminded the believer of the inaccurate legend that the sea was never to be seen off the Southport foreshore! The sea was to become the one who had the last laugh for many unwary souls.

## The Preston Rose Incident.

On the evening of the 28th August 1976 the twenty-foot-long, engine powered fishing boat The Preston Rose was launched into the sea at Southport. Aboard this vessel, looking forward to an overnight fishing trip was skipper Anthony Stanistreet, three other men and a boy. The sea was calm and there had been no forecast of anything unusual in the weather's behaviour for the period of the fishing expedition.

At the end of 1976 the hero No 10 Dukw of the Preston Rose incident comes to the end of its active service. The evidence of that service can be clearly seen. She was dismantled for parts and scrapped.

**Hero of the Preston Rose incident**

On the early morning tide of the 29th the engine of the Preston Rose roared into life and she turned her bows back in the direction of Southport. The crew settled down to reflect on their catch, tell stories of the ones that got away, and to sleep. They would be back on the beach within a few hours. Nearly half way home, the fortunes of both boat and crew took a change for the worse. Typical of the weather on this coastline a sudden storm arose of force seven dimensions, and the conditions soon had the small vessel plunging wildly in the heavy sea with breaking waves. The Rose had reached a position two miles West of Southport pier when she was struck by two giant waves, estimated to have been anything up to twenty feet high. These two towers of water swamped the boat and its engine. The crew frantically tried to bale some of the water, but their efforts proved unsuccessful. The Preston Rose was slowly sinking and at that point skipper Stanistreet fired two distress flares high into a darkening sky. The crew soon found themselves in the sea, remarkably cold even for August. Two of the crew could not swim and one was soon suffering severe cramp. Luckily, there were some hardy fishermen on the end of the pier that morning. They raised the alarm. The first vessel to go to the assistance of the doomed fishing boat and its endangered crew was the West Lancashire Yacht Club launch. It was soon struggling to make headway against a heavy sea. By now the Preston Rose was well down and the crew in the water waving for help, at 10.10am Sefton MBC D.U.K.W. No.10 rumbled from its base by Pleasure Land and into the sea. At the steering wheel was Ainsdale relief driver Alex Ventorini. There were also three lifeguards, the Assistant Chief Lifeguard, Bill Doherty, veteran lifeguard Frank Walsh and lifeguard Larry Nelson.

The red and yellow painted rescue vehicle, weighing just over two and a half tons, now battled against wind and sea for about thirty minutes. On arrival at the scene, with little hesitation, Bill and Frank jumped into the sea and between them helped the crew to the safety of the amphibious D.U.K.W. With all back on board they headed home. The channel which ran West to North of the pier in the 70s, was now in full flood and running at about six knots. The D.U.K.W. was being pounded by waves that broke over the vessel. The amphibians bilge pump system was working flat out to keep the vital engine power from being flooded by seawater. Bill Doherty had to decide to maintain their course to land South of the pier or try for the beach on the Northern side. He instructed the driver to turn North. At 11.10am the wheels of the D.U.K.W. hauled its weary passengers from the sea. The rescue had taken over an hour which meant the D.U.K.W, had nearly exhausted its supply of fuel. Though suffering from shock and exhaustion, the crew of the Preston Rose were otherwise in reasonable shape. They were given First Aid treatment and put under observation for three hours at the local hospital.

On inspection four hours later, the Preston Rose was found to have literally broken into four pieces, and the rescued crew after seeing the boat, admitted they were lucky to be alive.

**The Preston Rose Incident by the late Bert Orrit.**

Amateur artist and ex-Police Officer Bert Orrit in 1976 presented the lifeguards with this painting to commemorate the rescue. The crew of the Preston Rose funded the artist to paint the picture. It hung on the wall of the lifeguard's office on the Pleasureland car park. When the offices were demolished in the 1990s the painting ended up in a skip (hence scratch on right side). It was salvaged from the skip by local contractor, John Shacklady, and given to the author.

(Main text continues): The remainder of the decade of the 70s is a period again short on detail.

Records of the day to day activities of the Lifeguards and Sea Rangers have long since been lost and the only other detailed rescue, gleaned from a grateful letter from a teacher involved, was an incident that occurred in the month following that of the Preston Rose. In the September of 1976, on a warm summer's day on Ainsdale beach, a party of twelve school children and teachers from a small primary School near Manchester, were enjoying a walk towards the distant sea. The two teachers in charge had given the group advice on the hazards of beach conditions, but the party got split up, with the usual excited and adventurous charging ahead, and it soon became clear that two groups had strayed much too far. One concerned teacher went for help while the other went after the children. She crossed a mud bank, some twenty yards wide almost sinking up to the knees and then ran some distance to catch up with the first group. The now exhausted second group were suddenly unaware of the danger they were now in as the tide washed around their legs. To add to this, a dense sea mist began to envelope the stricken party. At the moment when visibility had fallen to a few yards making the situation critical for both children and teachers, a sound penetrated the dense, white haze. The growl of D.U.K.W. No 11s GMC engine announced the rescue vehicles' welcome appearance with the Assistant Chief Lifeguard aboard. The crew had spotted the group through their binoculars and picked up the other teacher. What the group did not know was that the mud channel had now filled up, cutting them off from the main beach. Only the powerful D.U.K.W. in full six-wheel drive, could plough through nature's deadly cocktail. The rescue D.U.K.W. returned the children and teachers to the safety of the First Aid hut where the teachers were treated for shock!

**Rescued Children**

The September 1976 school party incident. D.U.K.W. No.11 brings back a party of school children and teachers after being cut off by the incoming tide.

In 1979 Thompson and Doxey Export finally closed its door, and the repairs and maintenance of the D.U.K.W. fleet now passed into the hands of the Tourism and Attractions department of Sefton MBC. To help in this re-organisation Chris Trees, chief D.U.K.W. mechanic for Doxeys, was employed by Sefton, and he was to work in that capacity for the Council for several years.

The vehicles were now maintained at the bus depot used to service all the local Arriva buses used in the locality. This facility proved the best equipped to maintain the D.U.K.W. fleet. At the depot the maintenance schedule for each vehicle was broken down into short and long term stages. Each week, during the season, mechanics would travel down to the base on the Pleasure Land car park, paying special attention to the vehicles' wheel bearings and prop shafts. All the vehicles' oil and lubricant levels were checked as well as any unusual signs of damage, especially to the hull, prop shafts, propeller rudder, steering, tyres, etc. Due to the continuous problem of the braking systems, the handbrake was the only really reliable piece of equipment. The greatest enemy to any amphibious vehicle is the very conditions in which it was designed to operate. Thus, at the end of each season, the engineers of the Canning Road depot would grapple with the salt-based corrosion eating away at the limited life span of each D.U.K.W. although by present standards the D.U.K.W.s hull was made of strong steel, it still quickly showed signs of rust corrosion. These areas were removed and fiberglass and steel plates used to repair them.

**D.U.K.W. No 11 end of career**

Once the repairs were completed each vehicle was sent to the paint shop. There, at least three layers of Red Lead undercoat was applied to the D.U.K.W. in an effort to fight the corrosive forces of salt water, fine blown sand and erratic temperatures. Then the distinctive red and yellow livery of the Southport and later the Sefton Lifeguards was applied, then she was ready for another tough season. By the end of the 1970s and the early years of the next decade, replacement parts for the WW II veterans were becoming increasingly rare and thus increasingly expensive.

This became a real cause of concern, given the consumption of parts by each vehicle over the course of one year. The situation was made a little easier, however, by the build up of the spare parts stock each time a D.U.K.W. came to the end of its working life.

The cost of replacing one of the amphibians remained around £2,000 to £3,000 in the 1970s rising to around £10,000 in the early 1990s. Prices remained fairly steady for several years. As we shall soon see, however, even this positive financial situation was soon about to change for the worse.

In his very detailed reports, assistant chief Lifeguard Bill Doherty noted that the individual victims of the many incidents along that stretch of our shoreline, often came from right across the North of England. Equally varied, the situations and events which so overwhelmed them, that they called upon the skills of the Lifeguard Service. But there was always that common thread which tied together many of incidents the D.U.K.W. crews were called upon to handle, the unpredictable nature of the sea and the subtle dangers hidden from view in its murky depths.

### 1984 Season: Recorded Rescues Included...

APRIL: 1) 7 teenagers rescued. 2) 2 women/2 children trapped in vehicle. 3) 2 crew rescued from wrecked dinghy.

MAY: 1) 2 year old child/mother saved. 2) Horsebank; 4 in wrecked dinghy rescued.

JUNE: Total of 27 people who were cut off by tide, guided back to safety by the Southport D.U.K.W.

JULY: 1) 2 women saved from drowning. 2) Party of 5 rescued by D.U.K.W. 3) Cut off/ 2 adults and 2 children.

**AUGUST: 1) Party of day trippers/ cut off.**
Peak Aug Bank Holiday/21 vehicles stuck/one attempted suicide.

An important background fact concerning Bill Doherty's incident reports, (both handwritten and typed), was that these reports were not written for his own interest. These documents he passed on each week to his immediate superior, who in the 70s and 80s was Mr Phil King, director of Tourism and Attractions for Sefton MBC. In these reports Bill not only details the actual event, but records many details of those rescued. Once the summer season was rolling, folks from Lancashire, Merseyside, Yorkshire, etc flooded into town. Many of these visitors were without knowledge of the hazards of the North-West coastline and ignorant of the unpredictable moods of the sea. Behind the calm surface with its white breakers and slow tide, these visitors to our shores were drawn into a false sense of security. Some individuals were just un-informed and naive as to the nature of the shoreline. Others, more tragically, were saved by lifeguards as they attempted to take their own lives.

## Forced Landing - Waiting for the tide, Ainsdale.

21st Aug 1987. PC. Phil Gaskell on duty by the wrecked mail plane. Both Southport and Ainsdale Dukws.

### D. U. K. W. 19 and Plane Wreck

During the 1984 season Bill Doherty suggested to the Publicity and Attractions department the idea of a beach safety code. This would be a code of good safety practice on the beach for both adults and children. It could be promoted in schools and colleges, when they were visited by the Police or the Coastguard.

April/ Southport D.U.K.W. found two ladies and two babies trapped in a sinking car. They were half a mile from the pier. The tide had surrounded the vehicle, trapping them inside by blocking the doors. The Lifeguards dragged them all out through the windows. Vehicles never recovered.

**Lifeguards on Duty**

July/ A party of 5 people were seen about half a mile out opposite Weld Road trapped on a sandbank. Southport D.U.K.W. picked all 5 up, just as they were about to swim ashore across the channel. It is unlikely they would have made it in full flood. Same day eleven or twelve children and two adults had to be guided back from the area of Angry Brow, cut off by the tide!

1985 SEASON: RECORDED RESCUES INCLUDED…JANUARY: 2 men in sinking fishing boat.

MARCH: Men and dogs rescued from Horsebank. Two boys attempting to walk across the Channel.

MAY: Teenager attempted suicide.

JUNE: Party of 4 adults taken off Horsebank.

JULY: several vehicles trapped in sand/one with driver inside had to be rescued from incoming tide. Shrimping rig sank, owner rescued.

AUGUST: Within the first two weeks 17 people (including 5 children) removed from the danger of being cut off by the tide. Over half incidents D.U.K.W. crews were in attendance.

By the 1980s it was the policy of the Leisure and Tourism department of Sefton MBC to employ only a skeleton staff of Lifeguards during the closed season late September until April. The two chief Lifeguards Verdi Godwin and Bill Doherty would carry out the thousand and one maintenance jobs on the shore facilities that had come to their attention during the summer season. They were amongst the very few full-time employees. However, incidents along the shoreline were not uncommon in the winter. On a particularly bleak and wintery Sunday in the January of 1985 a report from a member of the public alerted the skeleton crew at the Foreshore office on Pleasure Land car park. A relative had taken out a 12-foot open boat on a fishing trip off Southport. There were three adults on board. Several hours had passed without word of their whereabouts. The available Lifeguards with Doherty in charge, prepared the standby D.U.K.W., but waited in case of a false emergency. Then a message from Crosby coastguard came through that the owner's car and trailer were still on the beach. By then it was late afternoon.

There was no full crew for the D.U.K.W. Bill and beach officer Chris Parkinson took a jeep along the beach and soon spotted the vessel a mile or so offshore. The three crew had been in the boat nearly seven hours consequently, they were now in a very distressed state with the engine broken down. All were suffering from hypothermia having been swamped by freezing waves and a sudden snow storm. Bill dived into the sea at the nearest point. He helped the three men to shore, one at a time. Then they were driven directly to the Southport Infirmary.

During that season some 36 individuals were rescued from being cut off by the sea, between Ainsdale and Southport. Again, five of these attempting to walk across the Ribble estuary to Blackpool!

By April of 1986 the weather had a summery early snap and this encouraged an equally premature influx of sun worshippers to the beaches. The Lifeguards and their amphibious vehicles were soon called upon. The first few weeks of the 1986 season had just managed to pass without event, when D.U.K.W. No.16, crewed by lifeguards Frank Walsh, Kevin Stringfellow and Assistant Chief Lifeguard Bill Doherty, answered the first of many incidents. A van had been spotted on a sandbank about half a mile from the end of the pier! The vehicle was being approached by the flood tide. On their arrival the Lifeguards found two adults and two dogs stuck inside the vehicle which was sinking into the sandbank. The victims were rescued through the windows, just before the tide washed over the stricken vehicle. All four were treated for shock, and the van sank without a trace! A few days later, but a few hundred yards from this incident, another emergency was answered by the same D.U.K.W. and crew. This time a party of fourteen individuals, on a day out in Southport, got trapped on a sandbank. They all had to be taken off together which proved to be a considerable squash!

The month of May in 1986 was a poor month weather-wise. Strong winds blew in from the South West. These conditions, however, encouraged the presence of Windsurfers. The Southport D.U.K.W. with Stringfellow, Tony Rigby and G. Jackson aboard diverted from its patrol. A surfer had last been seen in the notorious Bog Hole channel. Sure enough, clinging to his shattered board caught in the current, was the exhausted water sportsman. Tony Rigby dived into the sea while Stringfellow steered the red and yellow D.U.K.W. into a recovery position. The lifeguard, clutching the semi-conscious victim, was hauled to safety before both were swept away, but the rescue was not quite over yet. The powerful current now swept the D.U.K.W. onto a mud bank. It took some skilful forward and reverse action to get her off. The Lifeguards were forced to take the long sea route home.

The weekend of the 14th and 15th of May kept the crews of both the Southport and Ainsdale D.U.K.W.s busy. Incidents included the rescue of a twelve-year-old boy taken ill on a fishing boat. Another group rescue of seven adults from the Liverpool area marooned on the Horsebank and surrounded by the incoming tide.

Numerous vehicles stuck in soft sand.

The policy of trying to keep all the lifeguards in a constant state of peak physical condition to meet any situation was continued between incidents. Training was ongoing with the job itself. Drills and conditioning were organised enthusiastically by the two chief Lifeguards.

**D.U.K.W. Sefton Lifeguards Training.**

These lifesaving skills were practised on land and in the sea often in conditions which in today's world would have made the Health and Safety boys probably weep. In the July one incident illustrated the need for constant alertness. While Verdi Godwin was conducting a mock rescue exercise from the Southport D.U.K.W. some distance from the beach, a new Merlin Rocket 14-foot racing dinghy passed close by. Verdi observed that, instead of just two crew members the boat was supposed to carry, she had four aboard. Without any warning the dinghy was hit by a freak wave and capsized. All those aboard were thrown into the sea. The owner broke his wrist and his wife fractured her ankle. A mock rescue became the real thing. Luckily all were pulled aboard, with the Merlin sinking minutes later.

That month two eleven-year-old boys nearly drowned while playing near the Bog Hole Channel. One swept away on a plastic drum. One rescued hanging on to a drainage pipe in pitch darkness and on a rising tide.

AUGUST: Included two attempted suicides, man and woman in a violent domestic on the beach, 30 foot Catamaran, with three crew aboard, wrecked in the Pinfold channel.

SEPTEMBER: Woman mental patient involved Rangers, Police and rescue team in an incident along the Rainford's causeway at Crossens.

PHOTOGRAPH (Paul Schuck 1991)

**The Ribble Estuary**

Though, by the 1980s this stretch of water had long been redundant as one of the trade highways to Preston, as we have already observed in previous incidents, its presence still acted as a magnet to the uninformed or over adventurous. The illusion as to how easy it would be to stroll from Southport to Blackpool, created by the clear view of Blackpool Tower, was the trick. On a clear day, there lies Blackpool and St Annes, seemingly just a stroll across the sands! Oh how wrong a person can be! It was such an incident that kick started the 1987 season for the combined lifeguards and beach patrol. On the 1st of March of that year the season had still a month to go before Sefton's Lifeguards and D.U.K.W.s officially took up their stations. The two chief lifeguards, permanent Sefton employees, were working on repairs to the sea wall, when early in the afternoon three young boys were spotted several miles out walking to the Golden Mile. Alerted, the two lifeguards sent for the standby D.U.K.W., but ran across the sands. Having waded across the sluice outlet the three lads from Burnley were on the edge of the Estuary trapped on a mud bank, when the Lifeguards got to them. Apparently they had lost all their money in the arcades and were heading for the Trustee Savings Bank in Blackpool! I suppose they would be called valued customers?

The relationship between the D.U.K.W. rescue service, Sefton Department of Leisure Services and the Coastguard often prevented many a local incident turning into something much more serious. The presence of privately-owned fishing boats became an increasing hobby from the 1980s. This co-operation between the two organisations had thus also increased in importance. Hardly had the Lifeguards taken duty in 1987 when such an incident took place. They had just been equipped with a new D.U.K.W. No. 12, untried in any emergency. The Coastguard service sent a message to the Foreshore of a fishing boat drifting in heavy seas in the Pinfold channel. Chief Lifeguard Doherty, Walsh and Stringfellow responded. The new D.U.K.W. took nearly an hour to reach the vessel. Twice the powerful bilge pump system struggled to keep the water out, the problem caused by waves constantly braking over the vehicle. On their arrival the Lifeguard's found two very frightened 10 and 11-year-old boys and two adults.

The boat's engine had broken down. What was meant to have been an enjoyable fishing trip turned into a nightmare. The D.U.K.W. took them all back to the safety of the shore.

The continued diversity of the emergencies attended to by the beach patrol service illustrated during a busy 1987 season was that of the Canine call out. Two dog walkers with two dogs nearly lost their pets when they decided to run across the Mad Brow north of the pier. Owners marooned on bank while dogs leapt into the running channel. On the arrival of Lifeguards one wet and muddy animal victim leapt into the arms of one of the rescuers. In the same month over eleven children and adults (including one two-year-old) saved in the Bog Hole channel area.

Further Blackpool enthusiasts picked up in the estuary. In the last month of the season a light aircraft came down in the sea near the old, Rainford sand works and so Lifeguards and police were called to assist. On their arrival they observed the plane taking off (just) carrying not only the one person it was designed for but three. The plane, pilot and two passengers were last seen wave hopping towards Formby!

### The final year of the decade 1980s

The end of the 1980s showed no decline in the demands asked of the Sefton's guardians of the shoreline.

Indeed, quite the opposite. Despite the design, concept and construction of the D.U.K.W. rescue vehicles now being some 47 years old. they continued to be called out to the sort of emergencies which would test even a modern recovery vehicle.

However, as time would tell, behind the scenes the running costs and the issues of part replacements, were coming under greater and greater scrutiny.

By the end of the decade the motor car was becoming the issue around which many a dangerous incident would occur. Typical of these vehicle centred incidents happened on the Whit Monday of 89. Through the powerful binoculars issued to the Ranger service, just as the morning tide was in full flood, a car based situation began to unfold. Several hundred yards seawards of the pier, a car was spotted about to be swamped by the tide. There were signs that there were people still in the doomed vehicle.

By the time the Southport on duty D.U.K.W. and its crew arrived the water was well up the doors and the vehicle was fast settling into the mud. Trapped inside were two women AND two babies; one child of 6 and another of 12 months old. Trapped also in the mud and nearly up to the shoulders in water were the women's' two husbands who had been trying to get the doors open. The Rangers quickly attached the D.U.K.W.'s powerful winch to the car chassis and dragged the car out of the mud. The lifeguards levered a door open to get to the victims within.

One of the two children had been slightly burnt by the cars electrics shorting out. All were Transported to hospital for treatment and the vehicle was recovered though I doubt it ever saw the road again!

The season continued with mostly routine incidents until the first weekend in June. Then a call from the Crosby Coastguard station to the Pleasure Land Shore Rangers H.Q. alerted the Rangers to another vehicle based incident. The car involved was again off the Southport Pier Head. However, this vehicle was quite a distance further out! The Southport D.U.K.W. was at that moment on the southern most point of its patrol, approaching Rainford's causeway. By now all D.U.K.W.s had been fitted with radios. But the vehicle had to drive down the beach as fast as it could, at the same time avoiding the other cars and civilians who were now pouring onto the beach. Assistant Chief Lifeguard Bill Doherty leapt into the sea on arriving only to find the depth of the sea around the car was nearly six feet in depth. The owner was hanging onto the outside of his car. Doherty was a little surprised to find the gentleman in question was over 60 years of age. More surprising, inside the car was his three-year-old Grandson. Both very shaken victims were guided to the rescue vehicle.

The 23rd July 1989 broke the records for both good weather and visitors flooding into Southport. The beach was one of the main destinations for those visitors looking for sun, sea and back to back hazards! That day in 1989 was a record breaker also for the Sefton Sea Rangers.

Thanks to their presence, they helped prevent that day becoming a record disaster for both the town and the service. As the town sweltered in the afternoon heat, the eagled-eyed afternoon watch observed a not often repeated sight. A party of no less than 30 adults and children (plus two dogs) in trouble. This unfortunate gathering, 14 of whom were under the age of 8 years old, had decided to cross the Bog Hole Channel. This channel could be crossed at low tide in those days but at flood tide, the channel widens and the going underfoot becomes treacherous. With little time to spare the rescue team went into action. This rescue was going to be what was termed by the Rangers as a snatch! Literally drive by and drag aboard. The only real problem was that the D.U.K.W. was only designed to carry 16 adults in full combat gear! The rescuers, aware they only had time for one attempt, also became aware that this was going to be a record day of some description. As it was, things went okay. First aboard, wet and bedraggled, were the two dogs. One wanted to sit on the driver's lap. The remaining humans were in a similar condition, but luckily not all 30 wanted to join the dripping dog on the driver's knee. Crammed on every part of the D.U.K.W., they headed home! This, as it turned out, was also the first season for D.U.K.W. No. 19. A record breaking day all round and one that that party would not forget in a hurry.

Hardly had August got through its first week when the Rangers were summoned to another potentially tragic incident but a stones' throw from where they had carried out the record-breaking snatch. The infamous Bog Hole channel again became the centre of attention when walkers on the pier alerted the Lifeguards. D.U.K.W. No. 19 with Ranger P. Walker and Chief Doherty investigated and found a twelve-year-old boy trying to swim for help across the flooding channel. His mother had become stuck in a sump hole opposite to a water outlet in the Bog Hole. On arrival the two Rangers found her up to the waist in mud with the sea pouring into the hole. Together they dragged her clear with only seconds to spare.

Then they carried mother and son on their shoulders chest deep across the channel to the safety of the D.U.K.W. Though by no means the last incidents of the season, these two particular events, brought the 1980s to a dramatic conclusion.

We come to the 1990s and the final decade of D,U.K.W. based Sefton MBC rescue service.

These records are from the final reports written by Assistant Chief Lifeguard Bill Doherty. The reports for the decade of the 1990s season still only apply to the operation of the Ranger service at the Southport base. Regretfully, there are no such records for the operation of the Ainsdale vehicles. In some ways one might say we are getting only part of the story. However, going by the more extensive patrol area of the Southport D.U.K.W., it is the greater part of our account.

With opening of the 1990 season the D.U.K.W.s available for duty were vehicle Nos. 19, 20 and 21 with No.15 in reserve.

February. The need for all year-round availability of rescue units was still never more apparent. By February the skeleton staff covering the winter had already been called out to three life threatening incidents. The third of these, two miles from the sea wall opposite the pier head involving an elderly male walking his dog! Cut off by the channel flooding, in a gale force, Chief Doherty and Ranger Parkinson waded through a five-foot tide to bring both canine and human to safety. This very unfortunate trend of the owners of man's best friend leading both themselves and their beloved animals into easily avoided dangers, became an all too regular theme throughout the months

April to June.

The area around the Pier Head and the Bog Hole channel attracted the greater number of these mid- season incidents. In the 90s at low tide, the beach area under the end of the pier looked safe enough.

This appearance cloaked dangerous mud beneath the thin sand and a tidal current powerful enough to overcome the strongest swimmer.

Our animal friends, attended by their less beach aware owners, only account for a small number of close shaves. On the 10th of June, as the Southport D.U.K.W. began its patrol to the Horsebank, one of the Lifeguards onboard spotted through his binoculars a developing incident. Over in the infamous Penfold channel, three horses, their owners and traps were literally floating in the deepening water as they were being pushed down the channel out to sea. D.U.K.W. No. 20 moved rapidly into the channel. The crew were unable to load the horses onboard! Using the D.U.K.W. to protect horses and owners from the worst of the ebbing current, the group were guided to more solid sand where they could pull the traps to safety. Hardly had the D.U.K.W.s left this incident when a report came over the radio that the pilot of the Southport/ Blackpool Hovercraft (an unsuccessful venture), had radioed that a father and daughter were cut off by the tide a few yards from the last incident! No.20 turned back to sea. During those busy seasonal months of June and July, several more members of the public were spotted trying to walk from Southport on that all too familiar pilgrimage to distant Blackpool. That shimmering image of the tower on the horizon once again acted like a huge magnet.

On the 14th July two such visitors, exhausted after a mile or so, lay down on a sandbank and fell asleep. The tide then decided to flow in using its creeping silently mode. Luckily observed by people on the sea wall, a fifteen to twenty-minute dash by the Southport D.U.K.W. found them on a rapidly shrinking island! The couple, however, proved to be most anxious about the condition of their designer sportswear!

The safety of children continued to be an issue even into the 90s. In July a girl of six was found wandering alone on the Horsebank. She was taken to the police station, but even after several hours no one came forward to claim her. A young boy and girl from Kirkby, Merseyside walked out beyond the pier head. The girl then suffered an asthma attack. She fell into the sea. The boy attracted the attention of the D.U.K.W. on patrol by frantically waving and running up and down.

In November, two boys from a Lancashire children's' home, on a visit to Southport, sneaked off while their teacher was in the toilet!

Again, attracted by the distant lights of Blackpool, they set off for an adventure on the rides of the Pleasure beach and the Golden Mile. That was not to be of course. On reaching the Horsebank they both became stuck in a sump hole! As they sank up to their chests in thick mud, their growing plight came into vision through the binoculars of on duty lifeguards Alan Faulks and Kevin Stringfellow. Driving the D.U.K.W. at full speed, firstly across the sand, then through mud and finally into the incoming tide, they reached the two boys with only minutes to spare as the tide washed in over them. The Golden Mile did not look so golden that day for those youngsters. Their journey back in a World War II vehicle, however, was a perhaps some compensation especially when you consider what the alternative might have been! The 7th February 1991, after 34 years' service with first Southport Corporation and then Sefton MBC, Chief Lifeguard Verdi Godwin retired.

For his services to the beach patrol and Lifeguard service Verdi was awarded the British Empire Medal. On his retirement Deputy Chief Lifeguard Bill Doherty became Chief Beach Supervisor. He had already himself served twenty-five years on the D.U.K.W.s.

He had two Liverpool Shipwreck and Humane Awards and one Royal Life Saving Society Medal for Rescues for actions during those years.

On the weekend of the 26th May there occurred, again in the Penfold channel, a strange unexplained incident. Local shrimpers and fishermen are well known for their knowledge of the tides, sea conditions, sandbanks, hazards and unseen dangers. Indeed the Rangers and Lifeguards often used to exchange such information for the advantage of both groups. But the forces of nature can play tricks on even the most experienced. On that day, two miles out from the pier, D.U.K.W. No. 20 was near the outer limit of its patrol area. The D.U.K.W. crew noticed a shrimping Rig in trouble. The owner was waving for assistance. Shrimping Rigs are not small vehicles, they are built on the chassis and power units of heavy military lorries.

**Shrimp Rig Incident**
**This shows the size of a typical shimpers Rig.  (photo: G.Rimmer)**

These stand several feet above the tide line and are powered by engines that are in the higher horsepower category. This rig was sinking rapidly front first. The D.U.K.W. managed to reach the vehicle and haul the shaken owner aboard before it disappeared. It was literally swallowed up by a huge hole in the seabed! As if to confirm the mystery the following day, the 27th, an identical incident occurred. Two shrimpers rescued when their Rig sank down the same hole. There were, however, no further reports as to the origin of these strange incidents.

This clearly became known as the summer of strange events. That June, on a warm and pleasant weekday, Lifeguard Tony Rigby's focused on an unfolding incident. 23 children aged between 4 and 10, accompanied by one teacher, strolling out towards the Bog Hole channel near the wreck of the Chrysopolis of Genoa. The D.U.K.W., travelling at maximum speed, took about fifteen minutes to reach the party. All 23 from a junior school in West Yorkshire, were loaded onboard and then driven to the safety of the main beach. It was then discovered that 8 more children and 2 teachers were missing.

### Sea Mystery

Luckily, they were discovered further down the beach playing unawares of the narrow escape of the rest of the party. Following that on the 7th July, there were a further 13 individuals recovered one and a half miles out. This included three 12 year olds heading across the Estuary to, yes you have guessed it, once again those bright lights of Blackpool's Golden Mile!

The autumn of 1991 was the first year of Sefton's now very popular Air show. This new event caused a late season flood of visitors which did no damage to the local economy, but proved a little less popular with the coast Rangers. Ignoring the flags and warning notices, 25 individuals kept the Lifeguards on their toes as they proceeded to turn, what should have been an enjoyable weekend for all, into what could have been their last weekend!

Bringing the weekend to an uneventful end a very sleek new private yacht named The Wyvern grounded on the Mad Brow bank after its rudder broke in a sudden gale force wind. D.U.K.W. No. 21 took off all the four crew.

August witnessed further child center incidents. One of these on Whitsunday when nine victims, four aged between 7 and 12 years of age, were literally pulled out of the sea, an omen of things to come. The following weekend Lifeguards on the

Southport amphibian spotted a two-year-old child, on its own, about to walk into the incoming tide. Apparently, while her parents played a game of rounders, the youngster climbed out of her pram and went walkabout! The following day, an eighty year old grandmother and her young grandchild qualified for a ride in the rescue D.U.K.W. as they proceeded to get stranded off the sea wall. Meanwhile, also near to the seawall at the pier head, a family with 7 children were enjoying a picnic. It must have been good picnic as the parents or guardians did not notice the children going for a walk to the sea. The tide was, of course, again in full flood. Suddenly aware that their children were marooned on the seaward side, mother with baby in arms, dashed into the sea!

Disaster averted by the arrival of the patrol D.U.K.W. The report, however, does not mention the participation of the father in this family crisis. Up to the end of August this area around the pier head saw the rescue of a further nine children and eight adults. On the final day of that month, strong winds from the South West lifted the waves into breakers. Two windsurfers from Preston decided these were ideal conditions for them and launched out from the seawall. It was not long before one of the boards struck the concrete base of a 15 foot Storm water outlet. The board shattered into pieces. Its owner ended up clinging to the metal tower as huge breakers tried to batter him back into the sea. Two lifeguards, despite the conditions, swam to the tower to assist. Chief Doherty and veteran Ranger Frank Walsh ordered the standby D.U.K.W. to come to the incident. They joined in the rescue. Both Doherty and one of the other lifeguards were injured during this incident. The surfer was pulled aboard. All three end up at the Southport Infirmary. Within a few hours two more surfers had their masts broken and the D.U.K.W., with its reserve crew, returned to assist these extreme sportsmen.

October. Another out of season rescue and a further family tragedy averted. A family of four from Stockport, with their bikes, walked out to the Great bank. The two girls were aged 3 and 5. The flood tide surrounded them and lifeguards, alerted by a member of the public, waded to the frightened visitors.

## 1993 The Last D.U.K.W.

In that year the Lifeguards, and shore patrol became part of the Shore Rangers Service and all their equipment was re-organised in 1993 as part of a general departmental restructure by Sefton MBC. All the rescue services remained under the Leisure Services department.

D.U.K.W. Nos. 19, 20 and 21 were on the inventory. The restructure was an event which led to a close inspection as to the condition and future operations of the D.U.K.W. fleet. The Contract services department was given the task of assessing each vehicle at their depot. During this assessment of the fleet it was found that D.U.K.W. No. 19 was at the end of its working life and it could not be used for another season. It was earmarked to be dismantled for parts. The Leisure Services department wanted to continue the policy of having at least three vehicles available for the 1993/94 seasons. For that period the department's budget for the purchase and maintenance of rescue vehicles was £30,000. It was accepted that the purchase of a replacement vehicle would probably account for about a third of that budget. Though at the time the balance seemed adequate to maintain the fleet, the condition of both vehicles 20 and 21 carved a fair slice out of that surplus. However, the decision was made to go ahead and find another amphibian but to keep a much closer inspection of the fleet over the season.

Other out of season surprises still had a habit of rearing their ugly heads even for the now re-organised Lifeguard and coastal Rangers. The 7th of February saw a full-scale emergency involving the Rangers, Police and units of the Coastguard. At that time the few full time Lifeguards were doing off duty work on the pier. Conditions were very cold with a considerable sea mist which was drifting. There then appeared to be a bus on the beach flashing its headlights. On investigation it was found that the bus was from a Warrington children's home. Four girls aged 12 to 14 were missing as well as a male of 21 years suffering from a mental condition. A combined search, using a D.U.K.W. to sweep the shoreline took the three agencies over two hours. Search lights and parachute flares were brought into use to try and penetrate the sea mist. These efforts were rewarded by the safe recovery of all five individuals, who had managed to spread themselves out between the pier and the local R.A.F. aerodrome of Woodvale.

One of the earliest in season incidents in April was another horse rescue! Man's other best friend had managed to relieve itself of its rider. Then it decided to carry out a long-held dream and swim to Blackpool. Possibly it had some hay at the Blackpool TSB! The Southport D.U.K.W. rounded it up in true Western tradition. Between the months of April and September a total of 19 children (between 6 months and 14 years old), 22 adults, 3 dogs and 1 horse became members of that elite body of individuals who have rode the red and white (cream) D.U.K.W. amphibians. The circumstances for that journey were, however, far from enjoyable.

September: the second year of the popular Sefton Air Show. All Lifeguards leave was cancelled. The public did not let the Rangers down! Thirty-eight individuals helped to safety, twenty between the age of 10 and 15 years. Three more stuck on the Great Bank in their cars. Apparently the view of the planes was good as was that of the incoming tide which was about to cut them off.

I have already given reference to those hardy souls who shared the hazards of a life closely bound up with the sea along the NW shoreline, the local shrimpers and fishermen. Their presence goes back as long as the local history has been written. I have already mentioned also some incidents where the Fishermen and Lifeguards found themselves in each others debt. The 16th November was another such day.

With signals from a sinking shrimper's Rig seen north of the pier, the Sefton standby D.U.K.W. driven by D.U.K.W. driver Frank Walsh and crewed by Chief Lifeguard Bill Doherty and Kevin Stringfellow tried to tow it to safety. But even the D.U.K.W.'s powerful winch could not cope with the Rig's weight. At first the owner wanted to stay aboard but as his rig filled with water and sank the fishermen jumped from its roof onto the D.U.K.W. On the 19th November shrimper Joe Sumner also lost his rig despite the efforts of the Sefton D.U.K.W. and the Lytham Lifeboat. These vehicles often had much of their owners small income invested in them.

During the period of 94 to 95, the fate of the D.U.K.W.s as the guardian of the shoreline and its most charismatic champion Bill Doherty, were strangely intertwined. This was the last season Chief Doherty penned his reports. Ominously, the 94 season started early in the February. At that time of the year all the rescue D.U.K.W.s were undergoing their winter overhauls. A group of young motorbike enthusiasts, accompanied by three machines, were putting their bikes through their paces on the beach a half a mile from the sea wall. All were unaware of three muddy conditions on that area of the beach. It was not long before all the bikes were sinking and the tide moving in on the group. Equipped with a tractor, supplied by the coastguard, the few lifeguards available rode to the rescue!

During the following month 15 individuals, including 6 children from Walton, pulled from the sea and out of mud banks. These sudden bursts of activity, followed by periods of inaction, were the nature of the job of Lifeguard and. Sea Ranger. Again, after a temporary lull, June and July became awash in an avalanche of incidents. Some 60 children, between the ages of 1 and 13 years old, needed the assistance of the Rangers to get them to safety. The vast majority of these were with their families. In these incidents the adults themselves were often in as much trouble as their children. Their lack of awareness nearly lead to tragedy, but for the presence of the rescue service. Near the end of July seven children aged 8 years to 11 years old from a local stable decided to go for a swim off Southport, the sea that day was less than half a mile out. The party of youngsters were soon to become victims of freak weather conditions than can develop in no time. A sudden rainstorm descended. It was accompanied by thunder and lightning. With headlights and spotlights blazing both the Southport D.U.K.W. and the beach patrol jeep struggled through nearly zero visibility. The group were found nearly a mile offshore.

Three more shrimping rigs were lost during the last months of the season. These were the last records of the day to day actions and rescues carried out by the Sefton Lifeguards and the Beach Patrol.

**Sefton Chief Lifeguard William H. Doherty 1934 to 2009**

By 1995 Chief Lifeguard Bill Doherty had clocked up 32 years' service to the community of his adopted town of Southport. By that year, at the age of 62, Bill held the unique title as Britain's oldest Lifeguard. Even by that fateful year, the Chief Lifeguard could out swim and out run many of his junior contemporaries. By 1995 Bill held two Liverpool Shipwreck and Humane Society Awards and a Royal Lifesaving Award. He was credited with the saving of 461 individuals during his 32 years of service. On the fateful day of Friday 13th October 1995, Bill was called out on his final rescue. Out of season, with no D.U.K.W. available, a report came through of a lone woman in trouble on the Horsebank. The lady in question was a Green Party

Representative. Bill waded and swam to where she was marooned on the bank. His only way of getting her back was to carry her. This he did, in chest high water and a running tide. As Bill waded ashore he put his foot down a hidden hole in the sand. At first, he did not realise anything was wrong. But when he got home he collapsed on the floor. He had badly injured his back. After several weeks in hospital, the Chief Lifeguard in characteristic style fought his way back onto his feet. Many thought he would not walk again. But Bill's days in the uniform of the Lifeguards were over, it was the end of his career. From then on he devoted his time to continuing to help others at Southport Hospital Spinal Unit. He had, however, another battle of his own to fight. He developed cancer, which he fought uncomplaining, with only his close relations allowed the knowledge that he had the disease. He finally died at home on 19th November 2009. In the Annals of the History of Southport, Bill Doherty ranks as one of its greatest heroes.

1994. Jan. Sefton Purchases its Last Dukw To be No. 22.

D.U.K.W. No 22 coming out of its paint preparation shop. The first in the new Sefton Yellow/red Livery.

## Last D. U. K. W.s

By 1994 Sefton Rangers D.U.K.W.s Nos. 20 and 21 were in a serviceable condition, but No19 was now scrapped. At this point, Mr David McAleavy who now led the Coastal Management Team, recommended the replacement of No.19 with one last D.U.K.W. A possible replacement vehicle was then on the premises of Hewitt Engineering, the main supplier of D.U.K.W. parts to Sefton MBC. A deal was struck and the last vehicle purchased. This was to become No 22 vehicle, the last of the fleet. In the same year, other forces were at work. The rising cost of the forty-year War Veterans was becoming such a fact of life that few could ignore it. For instance, in 1994, the estimated budget for overhauling D.U.K.W.s Nos. 20 and 21 for the 94/95 season was £6,513. The actual cost came to £13,800.

During the 1995 season there were a few plans of returning redundant vehicles to the Tourism and Attractions dept. to carry passengers on beach trips. The Health and Safety committee, however, had other ideas, and they identified many areas which could not be covered. The D.U.K.W.s could not be brought up to be safe enough condition to carry passengers without considerable investment. In a memoranda Chief Tourism and Attractions Officer Phil King expressed his hope that at least one vehicle could be kept in Southport as a token of their participation in the town's history. Nothing, however, came of these expressions of regret at the coming redundancy of the historic Sefton D.U.K.W.s.

In December of 1996, the Director of Sefton Leisure Services submitted a report to the Leisure Services Committee entitled 'Whether to extend the lease for the D.U.K.W.s on Southport beach or dispose of them and pay up the leases (1296)."

**1995 Officials**
**The mayor and council officials visit the Lifeguards. DUKW 21 is in the**
**final livery of the Sefton Lifeguards. The uniform too is the last of the**
**service as the end is in sight.**

This was the first official move to end the vehicles' service. The main rationale for retiring the D.U.K.W.s and using a new vehicle was the ever increasing cost of keeping the war veterans serviced and functioning. By 1995, the report states, the annual bill per vehicle had reached a staggering £10,000. Breakdowns were becoming a regular event together with the increased shortage of spare parts, problems with the braking units and breaches of the safety standards code. These were just a few of the concerns, supported by the Vehicle Maintenance Section. While recognising the past service of the D.U.K.W., it recommended decommissioning the last D.U.K.W.s, then two options would be available.

Offer for sale…there had been a number of enquiries by interested individuals and organisation.

The vehicles be offered to the local (now defunct) Transport Museum for possible display as a tourist attraction.

The Leisure Services Dept was now faced with the problem of a possible vehicle to replace the D.U.K.W. What is rather interesting is that this report was given in the December of 96, yet in the July of the same year tests on a replacement vehicle, THE SEACAT (later Supacat), had already taken place. The reports on its suitability as a replacement were glowing, though in retrospect, maybe just a little too positive.

Supacat

The initial trials of the Supacat 6x6 all purpose terrain vehicle actually took place on Southport beach on the 25th July 1996. These were conducted under the supervision of the Coast and Countryside Service for Sefton MBC. Present were council representatives of the Leisure Services dept, the Technical Services dept, the manufacturers of the Supacat LTD and Traction Equipment Ltd as well as members of the Lifeguard staff. These trials formed the basis of a recommendations forwarded to the Leisure Services committee, the Coast and Countryside Service and to the Southport MP Councillor John Pugh. This report basically set out the case for the retirement of the D.U.K.W. as the main rescue vehicle and its immediate replacement by the Supacat.

After the trials, the Supacat's performance results were compared with that of the WW II D.U.K.W. As well as the previously mentioned issue of the veterans increasing maintenance costs, the comparison included:

The inability of using the D.U.K.W. on any public roads mostly due to constant brake failure. The Supacat was also a road vehicle.

The D.U.K.W.'s slower reaction time compared to the Supacat.

The Supacat could be available for all year. The D.U.K.W.s were out of action from October to April undergoing their major winter overhaul.

The Supacat performed more positively in soft sand and mud than the D.U.K.W. It was able to get to parts of the beach (e.g. dunes, mud banks) inaccessible to the D.U.K.W.

**D.U.K.W. 20/22 in the final Sefton lifeguard colour scheme.**

The D.U.K.W.s, during the 1996/97 season, broke down on average once every 11 days. A situation made worse by a shortage of spare parts. The Supacat used standard parts from Landrover and Volkswagen and thus it was hoped that the maintenance costs would be much lower.

The report recommended that the D.U.K.W.s should be phased out in the 1997 season and that one Supacat be purchased subject to seventeen modifications which proved necessary during the trials. The cost quoted to the Leisure Services in January 1997 was £41,194 per vehicle with a further £2,803 of modifications for beach operations (e.g. marine paint for Sefton livery, flashing beacon lights, adjusting headlights, additional spotlights, delivery and crew training etc.). Thus the Supacat would serve briefly alongside the D.U.K.W.s for the rest of the 1997 season.

By the autumn of 1997 vehicles Nos. 20 and 22 spent their final days in the new livery of the Sefton Leisure Services lying in the yard of the old Council offices in Formby. Their future fate now sealed with the statement in the minutes of the Leisure Services submitted to the Sefton council meeting of 29th January.

To the Economic Development and Tourism (General Purposes) sub- committee.

That the option 1 to dispose of the D.U.K.W.s be approved.

They were part of the Dept. of Leisure Services
20 seen without weather covers and 22 with.

**Warning hailers removed from side of screen**

The Leisure Services committee be informed that this sub-committee view that expressions of interest should be invited for the disposal of the D.U.K.W.s, subject to a reserve price reflecting the future purposes for the use of these vehicles."

With this statement of intent interest in vehicles Nos. 20 and 22 was canvassed.

Not surprisingly there was no shortage of response from museums, private restoration concerns and professional bodies. By the April of 1998 both vehicles and all spare parts had been disposed of. No. 20, in a non-running condition, had been purchased for just £1,101 by a private restorer in Heysham. D.U.K.W. No. 22, however, being in running order, was purchased for £4,000 by Hewitt Engineering of Leicester. The same Hewitt Engineering who had sold it to Sefton in 1996! There was to be a final ironic twist to the story.

The year 1998 brought the Final Period of the U.S. amphibious World War II D.U.K.W. service on the beaches of Southport and Ainsdale to its final close. Events elsewhere in Britain, however, were to prove that the now ageing amphibian was not going to drive into the sunset. At least, not quite yet!

# CHAPTER SEVEN

# OLD D.U.K.W.s NEVER DIE;

They Just Become "QUACKER DUCKS!"

After the purchase by Hewitt Marine of Southport D.U.K.W. No 22 in 1998, there were no further plans to commemorate the service of the Lifeguards and the six hundred odd lives they had saved. It looked as if the presence of the World War II veteran was now well and truly confined to the pages of history. Events elsewhere, actually in the nations capital no less, was about to herald a Renaissance in the public career of the D.U.K.W. A Renaissance which would have its origins in the adventures and imagination of Routledge and Rankin in those early days of the 1950s in Northern England.

In the United States the idea of a further extension to the D.U.K.W.s military career was already blossoming hardly before the ink on the WW II surrender documents had dried. Hundreds of war surplus D.U.K.W.s were signed off by the United States government together with plentiful supplies of spare parts. The D.U.K.W.s revolutionary qualities were not lost on the creative American public. From 1945 onwards D.U.K.W.s began to surface in the livery of such organisations as the Fire Service, the River Police, the Coastguard and wherever its combined land and sea-going skills could be exploited. There seems just a little hint of irony that, while Routledge and Rankin's yellow and red amphibians were entertaining holiday makers in austerity post war Britain, identical plans were being developed across the Atlantic. In the state of Wisconsin, close to the city of Milwaukee, a certain Mel Flath was one of the first to open a company in the US using D.U.K.W.s as a recreational vehicle. With his small family concern Dell Army Ducks, he laid the foundations of a river tour business that proved so popular that it lasted for many years. Following Dell Army Ducks, other ventures sprang up across the continental U.S.A. but one in particular was to have a profound influence on the story upon which this section of my book is based. In the spring of 1994, in the New England city of Boston, the Boston Duck Tours company first opened for business and they used as their base the Charles River rather than the unpredictable currents of the nearby ocean. In their first season The Boston Duck Tours company had only one vehicle which they named "BEANTOWN BETTY" after the nickname given to their fair city by the crews of the great sailing ships of old.

BOSTON 1966. ONE OF THE CITIES DUCK TOUR VEHICLES. THE IDEA WAS TRANSPORTED AND RECREATED IN THE LATE 1990s TO THE LONDON THAMES. AS WE HAVE SEEN, THE IDEA WAS NOT ORIGINAL. JUST UPDATED!

(PHOTO: K. STRINGFELLOW)

### Boston D. U. K. W.

The business quickly grew and with it the company as more vehicles were added to the inventory.

In the late 1990s a British holiday maker stepped aboard one of the Boston Ducks for his tour of the city and river. Professor of Biology Howard Slater enjoyed this D.U.K.W. experience so much, he became converted to the whole idea of the use of the D.U.K.W. as a vehicle for public recreation in Britain. As sure as one can be, he appears to have had no knowledge that the idea had already been exploited in his own country nearly five decades previously. An inspired Howard Slater then returned to the UK and began to search for financial backing for a duck tour business. He managed to secure a base for this venture on a small stretch of the River Thames. Finally, the first London Duck Tour company was founded, but like any new ducklings, the company was to face many challenges before it could take to the water! To secure such a prestigious base took many, many months of work. Especially difficult for the new organisations was how to fit each duck journey into the very complicated traffic movement on the already busy ancient river. The Port of London Authority and the Guild of Watermen had to be satisfied that the presence of the amphibious vehicles in the Thames, would not upset the flow of the established traffic or be a danger in any way. Before any craft can negotiate the River Thames, hundreds of years of tradition and rights of passage must be observed.

London Thames Tour (permission London Duck Tours)

The capitals' first D.U.K.W. tour operation, given the rather amphibious title of The London Frog Tours company, now had the task of building their business based on a vehicle which had ceased its military career over fifty years before. Even the British army had retired most of its fleet around 1974. This task, however, was made easier by the presence in this country, at that time, by two military vehicle firms upon whom the job of supplying such vehicles was an expertise they had acquired over years of experience. The Frog Tours company first turned to Rex Ward to help with the 5 vehicles they needed to bring their plans to fruition. He was able to negotiate the purchase of three vehicles which had been in service with the French Army. Many of these machines were part of the American Lend Lease Scheme and when their service careers came to an end they were put into storage.

Next, Hewitt Engineering of Barrow on Soar, Leicestershire, the very company that purchased Southport D.U.K.W. No. 22, brought 2 vehicles over from Holland to add to the fleet. It is more than possible, though records are not available to say with one hundred per cent certainty, that Southport D.U.K.W. No. 22 also found its way into the Frog Tours company. Regretfully, Hewitt Engineering has now ceased trading and any possible record of such a transaction are lost. To bring a WW II vehicle up to an acceptable mechanical condition to pass its Public Service Vehicle Standard Certificate is by no means an easy proposition. Any vehicle wanting to travel on the Thames for the purpose of business which involves members of the public, must carry this document. For the new Thames Duck Tours company an added complication was that their vehicles must equally be governed by regulations covering their movement on both land AND water because of the 75 minutes taken by each D.U.K.W. trip, over half of that time was to be spent on the busy roads of the capital. In 1999 permission was granted for the D.U.K.W. company to construct a purpose built concrete ramp into the Thames near Vauxhall Bridge. This construction, which enabled the tour company's vehicles to make a spectacular entrance into the River Thames via a huge wave, was built on land acquired from the Duchy of Cornwall.

**London D. U. K. W. Conversion (permission London Duck Tours)**

As for the many alterations to the D.U.K.W.s themselves, too numerous and complicated for a duff-handed mechanic like me to explain, one can only say that the D.U.K.W.s old GMC engines were not allowed to pour the fumes of untreated petrol onto the good citizens and visitors on London's streets. Instead low sulphur power units, such as the Bedford 330 two and a half litre six cylinder engine was installed. Health and Safety required that the 30 passengers be in a completely enclosed environment with a comfortable seating arrangement for each person. Improved access to the rear of each vehicle was required as it was considered inappropriate for passengers to scramble up the sides, a feat only fit for GIs and Lifeguards! The new rear access also had to remain watertight when the loaded D.U.K.W. ploughed through the strong currents of the Thames river. The safety equipment was issued to each vehicle continued the theme of the safety of all who would make the journey along the water highway of Britain's capital city. With the time spent during each excursion being divided by transportation on both land and water, all aspects of the vehicle's propulsion system, steering mechanisms and braking units would come under detailed scrutiny before the vehicles could be allowed access to the river Thames.

The pressures of pioneering such a revolutionary idea in the tourist industry soon took its toll on the young Frog Tours company. With the new millennium underway, the Thames tour company came under new management with a new title of London Duck Tours. By 2017 the London Duck Tours company were still very much in the business of introducing yet another generation to the unique amphibian. This activity is carried out through a series of their leisure and educational tours. London Duck Tours operate pretty well all the year round, though there is a reduced service during the winter months. These tours depart from Belvedere Road, Waterloo, in London SE1.which is close by the famous London Eye. (between the Jubilee gardens and the Southbank Festival Hall).

Around the same time there were similar ventures one of these in Dublin and another in Glasgow. Of these two, the Dublin D.U.K.W. company, still operates under the title of Dublin Viking Duck Tours. Again, in 2017 this Dublin based venture was gearing up for a new season. Its 75 minute tour of the cities sites, including St. Patricks cathedral and Dublin Castle, starts in spectacular fashion with a splash entry into the Canal dock! The land and water tours run 7 days a week from March to October, then weekends November to December. In those early years of the new millennium, a group of former personnel of Frog Tours moved north to the city of Liverpool. This choice of venue was, in itself, a strange twist of fate being the home of one of the founders of the D.U.K.W. tour idea in the 1940s John Routledge. The Liverpool Yellow Duck Marine Company opened for business in the April of 2001. They had but two vehicles in their fleet in those early days, both WW II veterans with the chassis numbers 35319572 and 35320332. The first of these two machines was originally owned by the oil giant BP where it spent several years working for them in Aberdeen harbour. It was then sold to a museum but was never displayed, finally it was rescued by Rex Ward one of this country's foremost authorities on the WW II amphibian. Rex used this vehicle to test out a theory he had about the possible conversion of the vehicle's power to a more cleaner and efficient engine. He used the Bedford 330 diesel engine in the test bed D.U.K.W. and in 1997, to prove the conversion a real winner, drove the vehicle from the UK to the Costa Brava! This breakthrough now opened the gates to the possibility of more similar conversions and the future expansion of the use of D.U.K.W.s in the modern tourist industry.

The newly formed Yellow Duck Marine Company opened their offices and repair facilities, firstly in Jordan Street but in 2005 they moved to Grafton Street. The company business premises were situated at the Albert Dock complex in the Atlantic Park Warehouse. Just like their fellow duck companies in London and Dublin, at the end of every hour-long tour of the city and the old docks passengers are treated to a rather spectacular splash entry into the murky waters of the Salthouse Dock!

**Q2 Spashdown**

As with the experience of the London Duck Tours Company, the vehicles of the new Liverpool concern had to go through a similar metamorphosis before being allowed by Liverpool City Council to be a regular feature on the city's streets. The fleet of vehicles quickly grew with the first vehicle added in 2006, then number 4 in 2009 and then in 2012 a vehicle to be converted to Quacker Duck 5 was purchased. The conversion of the military D.U.K.W. is indeed a very skilled job especially when faced with the regulations laid down by the government bodies and the departments of local government. This task grew ever greater as the supply of available machines dried up. In 2012 an event in the City of Liverpool brings me to the subject of the second even more famous individual (well actually its two individuals) to grace the decks of the WW II hero. As part of her Diamond Jubilee celebrations Her Majesty the Queen and Prince Philip paid a memorable visit to the City of Liverpool and on that day they took a ride in a Quacker D.U.K.W. of the Yellow Duckmarine Company!

In the June of the following year 2013, a series of unforeseen disasters then struck the Liverpool company! With 33 passengers onboard, the same vehicle sank in the same Salthouse dock! Thankfully, everyone aboard was picked up by the prompt action of the emergency services and the training of the duck's crew. This incident, however, followed a similar one that occurred a few months earlier. Public confidence was dented in the duck tours, despite a long period of reliable service. Concerned voices arose as to the safety of the amphibious vehicles. The result was, the end of the popular Yellow Duckmarine company.

Their presence on the Liverpool waterfront was sadly missed.

**Permission Trinity Mirror**

# CHAPTER EIGHT

# BEFORE WE DRIVE INTO THE SUNSET...

Dealing with a story that has had its share of twists and turns which have surprised the author, one more of these little gems was about to jump into the pages! In October of last year, when the main part of the research for this book was complete, I received a surprise email from Rod Elgey from Windsor in Berkshire. The email concerned one of the last three D.U.K.W.s to be employed by Sefton MBC on the beaches, vehicle number 21. According to my few records of this vehicle, it went to scrap as its condition on retirement was worse than poor! Rod had seen an article I had written on the internet back in 2010. He informed me that, up to that point the information was correct but the story of number 21 had not stop there. After departing to Manchester from Southport, to be scrapped, the new owner was rather taken by the D.U.K.W. and decided to have a go at a spot of restoration. Using the company crane, he hoisted the old D.U.K.W. upside down, still with all its running gear and fittings. This was to give him access to the condition of the hull. At that point there appears to have been a systems failure!

The crane broke and the already rust encrusted number 21 plunged to the ground causing further damage. The end of a restoration project for one individual, however the vehicle's luck had not yet run out. Knowledge of the wreck, warts and all, came to a Mr Peter Taylor of Consett, County Durham. Peter now purchased the ex-Southport amphibian, again with an eye to scrap value, and transported it back to his fascinating workshop. As a highly skilled fitter and welder, Peter eyed the battered number 21 realising its extreme state of health. But the old D.U.K.W. magic worked its spell and 11 years ago Peter Taylor began the long task of returning D.U.K.W. 21 to its former glory all by himself. Now, the long task is gradually coming together, though there is still much to accomplish. The vehicle has been completely stripped and rebuilt. During this huge task even sand from the old Southport days was discovered inside the chassis. If ever there was an appropriate tale to end a tale, this is it. After all, together it is only like taking A D.U.K.W. TO WATER!

D. U. K. W. 21 Renovation

From the depths of nowhere this could be either D.U.K.W. 20 or 22 both survived the axe when the service was terminated. As one will read, the 2016 auction house Brightwells catalogue had the vehicle on its books, including some documentation which I have tried to obtain details.

Thursday, January 9, 2020 Southport Visiter

# 'Duck' that kept our beach safe up for sale

BY JAMIE LOPEZ
jamie.lopez@reachplc.com
@jamie_lopez1

AN AMPHIBIOUS WWII truck which went on to patrol Southport beach is going under the hammer.

Auction house Brightwells is selling a unique piece of the town's history in the form of the 1945 DUKW amphibious truck.

The red and yellow vehicle was a familiar sight on Southport's beaches and is credited with saving 600 people in its working life.

Colloquially known as the "duck", the vehicle was designed in weeks and was used to transport troops and supplies to invasion battlefields and extract wounded soldiers.

The six-wheel-drive vehicle featured a watertight hull and propellor and featured a top speed of 50mph on land and 5.5 knots on water.

Weighing 6.5 tons and measuring 31ft long, 8ft 3in wide and 7ft 2in high, it pioneered the use of tyres whose pressure could be varied from inside the cab depending on the terrain.

More than 21,000 of them were made by the end of the war and a few remain in service to transport tourists or cargo in swamps and rain forests.

The model on sale was manufactured towards the end of the war in April 1945 and was restored in France in 1963 where it had been in service with the French military.

In 1974 it was imported to the UK from Belgium and then entered service as a beach patrol vehicle in Southport until the 1990s.

Having spent the past 28 years under cover as part of a large private collection, the vehicle is still in running order and is listed with a sale price of £18,000.

The listing says: "Pleasingly, it retains much of its original equipment including a full set of hood frames, the remains of the canvas hood, winch, anchor, hand bilge pump, surf dodger and crank handle.

"A set of English language data plates are also included along with a new set of side-protector strips, while a spare set of wheels and tyres will be made available to the new owner by separate negotiation if desired. Documentation includes the aforementioned dating letter, import documents and correspondence file, plus a copy of an original US military 'operational procedures' manual and a 72-page book on the DUKW by ISO Publications.

"With only a few dozen ducks still surviving worldwide, this marvellous machine has great commercial potential and is sure to cause a huge amount of interest wherever it goes.

"Given that the last two

An article from the Southport Visiter by Jaime Lopez was published dated Thursday January 9th. 2020.

# **Bibliography**


1949 Southport Botanic Gardens Museum J.H. Lawson Booth. History of Southport Lifeboats.

February 1944: war department technical manual. TM9- 802.Ordnance Supply Catalog. (ORD 7-8-9) Truck 2and a half ton. Two and a half ton 6x6 Amphibian Truck (GMC D.U.K.W. 6x6, Amphibian. Army Service Forces Oct 1944 D.U.K.W. 2 and a half ton 6x6 Amphibian: Geoff Pleasance: ISO Publications 1978.

Outlines MY1 Amphibious vehicles: Jeff Woods: Outline publications.1983.

D.U.K.W. Trials: John Havers: ISO Publications. 1989

GPA/D.U.K.W. Walk Around Colour Series: David Doyle: Signal Squadron Publications. 2015

The Cuttings Collection of the Late Joseph Rankin RNR: 1949 to 1957. (private collection)

The Daily reports of the Southport/ Sefton Chief
Lifeguard the late William Doherty. 1955 to 1990 (private collection PRD)

**1990s The Last Patrol**

# <u>**Appendix:**</u>

**COMPANIES WHO ARE RUNNING D.U.K.W. /DUCK TOURS UP TO 2019**
**(USA/UK and Ireland)**

The author has endeavored to make the list as accurate as he can, but apologizes for any details that might have changed or are now out of date.

**THE UNITED KINGDOM (GB)**

**WINDSOR DUCK TOURS**

    (includes also the river Thames)

www.windsorducktours.co.uk

UK code: 01753-581158

**REPUBLIC OF IRELAND Viking Tours of Dublin**

    (Tour of the Irish capital land/water)

info@vikingsplash.ie

Dublin D12 HD68

**THE UNITED STATES of AMERICA**

**TEXAS : GALVESTON DUCK TOUR**

    (Home of the publication D.U.K.W.s to WATER!)

ducktours@comcast.net

+1   409-621-4771

**AUSTIN DUCK TOURS**

    (tours of land and lake)

https://austinducks.com

+1  512-477-5274

**D.C : WASHINGTON DC DUCK TOURS**

    (includes the Potomac river)

+1 866-754-5039

bookings can be by Viator

**MASSACHUSETTS: BOSTON DUCK TOURS (established 1994)**

(25 years of a wide range of tours and amphibious experiences.)

bostonducktours.com

+1  617-267-3825


**VERMONT: MAINE DUCK TOURS (PORTLAND)**

(1 hour historical land and sea tour)

+1 207-774-3825


**WASHINGTON STATE: RIDE THE DUCKS OF SEATTLE**

(Land and water tours)

ridetheducksofseattle.com

+1  206-441-3825


**CALIFORNIA: SAN DIEGO SEAL TOUR**

(90 minute land and sea tours)

www.sealtours.com

+1 619-298-8687


**ALABAMA:MOBILE GULF COAST DUCK TOURS**

(Triple splash!)

info@gulfcoastducks.com

+1 251-525-6933


**FLORIDA: MIAMI BEACH DUCK TOURS**

(Includes Biscayne Bay)

ducktourssouthbeach.com

+1 305-673-2217


**WEST PALM BEACH VIVA DUCK TOURS**

(Using the new Hydra-Terra vehicle)

divaduck.com

+1  561-844-4188

**WISCONSIN: DELLS DUCK TOURS**

   (Founded 1946/ uses original D.U.K.W.s)

wisconsinducktours.com

+1    608-254-8751


**RHODE ISLAND:  ROGER WILLIAMS PARK**

   (Providence)  DUCK TOURS

 (authentic WW II D.U.K.W.s)

providenceriverboat.com

+1 401-785-9450


**ALASKA: KETCHIKAN DUCK TOUR**

   (All family fun experience)

www.experienceketchikan.com

+1  907-225-9899

A Legend Departs the Water into History

9 781590 954706